Reflections on Medicine:

Essays by

Robert U. Massey, M.D.

Reflections on Medicine:

Essays by

Robert U. Massey, M.D.

Edited by

Martin Duke, M.D.

Gordian Knot Books

An Imprint of Richard Altschuler & Associates, Inc.

New York

Reflections on Medicine: Essays by Robert U. Massey, M.D.

For information contact the publisher, Richard Altschuler & Associates, Inc., at 100 West 57th Street, New York, NY 10019, RAltschuler@rcn.com or (212) 397-7233.

Library of Congress Control Number: 2010929556
CIP data for this book are available from the Library of Congress

ISBN-13: 978-1-884092-98-5
ISBN-10: 1-884092-98-5

Gordian Knot Books is an imprint of Richard Altschuler & Associates, Inc.

Text Design and Layout: Wanda E. Jacques-Gill

Cover Design and Layout: Josh Garfield

Printed in the United States of America

Table of Contents

Foreword

I HAVE been spending hours at a time recently, rereading a decades-long correspondence with Bob Massey. Those hours have gently welcomed me back to earlier times, when Bob was alongside me in person almost as much as we were together figuratively in the pathways of life. Men are not very good at expressing affection for other men, but Bob and I did somehow manage it, in so many ways that gave voice to our understanding of each other.

In my pilgrimage through the many evocative sheets of stationary which at this moment lie before me, I came across a note I sent to Janet Massey in September 2004, when I still had three more years to accompany Bob on the journey we had long been taking together. The second sentence reads as follows: "My almost 30 year friendship with your father has been a beacon for my life." And so it has, even now when he is elsewhere or nowhere.

I choose those last three words advisedly, because they epitomize a philosophical and religious quest on which Bob embarked long before his earthly life ended, that motivated him until his final hour. The last book he held in his hands, only a very short time before his death, was written by a man whose career and spiritual seekings were much like his own. The slim volume was Sir William Osler's 1904 Ingersoll Lecture at Harvard University, *Science and Immortality*, a disquisition in which the greatest of medical America's inspirational figures grappled with his conjectures on the existence of an afterlife, invoking classical and more recent scholarly texts whose contents, by the late 20th century, could be appreciated only by the few remaining Massey-like thinkers who were thoroughly familiar with them and with their deepest meanings.

As Robert Unruh Massey pondered such inscrutabilities—in the same way he applied his massive erudition to so many other themes universal and specific—he accepted the uncertainty of human wisdom and even knowledge, recognizing that it is for each generation to look anew at dilemmas both modern and ancient. He not only did not shrink from such challenges, he welcomed them with the enthusiasm of catalyzed curiosity and the unmitigated joy of the autodidact who bases his searchings on an already-acquired broad base of understanding. Unruh—German for restlessness—was literally his middle name. Even his own vast horizons of understanding were not sufficient to satisfy his unquenchably questing nature; he sought always to widen them, not only for himself but for others.

We are those others. Whether we are among the fortunate ones who benefited for so many years by reading his monthly essays during the 15 years when Bob wrote them from the University of Connecticut as "Reflections from the Dean's Office" and later when he was the Editor of *Connecticut Medicine* as "Reflections on Medicine," or are being introduced to them in this representative collection assembled with such devotion by Martin Duke, they are ours now. They cover a broad range of topics, and yet they represent only a modest example of those issues to which Bob put his figurative shoulder. In these pages, he speaks to us of philosophical and practical matters, of issues direct and abstract, of his literary and medical heroes alive and long gone, of cabbages and kings. His soothing voice is always modulated in that engaging and enlightening manner that characterized every form of discourse in which he took part, whether verbal—as in speeches, conversation, or his gifted teaching of students, colleagues and general audiences—or written—as in essays, letters and published papers. The phrases are felicitous, immediate and accessible; he had a way of speaking simply of the most profound and often abstruse topics; he made his case *in*ductively and clarified it *de*ductively. As every new reader will soon find for herself or himself, he was an explicator of conundrums and complexities. He was, in short, a master teacher.

The world of medicine, the world of thought, the world of the humanism he brought to his every pursuit—are all lessened by Robert Massey's absence. I keep a framed photograph of him less than five feet from my fingers and mind as I work, to remind me that such people can exist, and to remind me of my love for him. In one of the letters he wrote to me in the last period of his life, he said, referring to his adored wife of more than 60 years who had died in 2005, "I'm sure my greatest desire is to be again with June. Whether life is immortal and we may be back together, I won't learn until and if I get there!" The skepticism of his Science said no, but the depth of his Faith said yes. In either case, he is immortalized in this small book, and in the minds of the multitude who will be added to the privileged list of those blessed to have been his acolytes. May the memory of him continue to inspire the angels of our better nature.

Sherwin B. Nuland, April 2010

Introduction

BETWEEN 1973 and 2005, the late Robert U. Massey wrote more than 300 essays for *Connecticut Medicine: The Journal of the Connecticut State Medical Society*, examining many important issues about the practice, philosophy, and culture of medicine. Some of his "Reflections" were written while he was dean of the University of Connecticut School of Medicine, others while he was editor or editor emeritus of the Journal. All demonstrated remarkable scholarship, insight, and literary qualities that were greatly admired by the Journal's readership. "His was a quiet eloquence"[1] it was once said of the physician, writer and editor Joseph Garland, a phrase that seems equally well-suited in describing the writing of Bob Massey.

It was my good fortune to have known Dr. Massey when I taught at the medical school, attended his seminars on medical history, and served on his editorial board at the Journal. After he died, it seemed to me that his essays might well be gathered into a single volume, not only for the interest of those who had appreciated them in the past but also for the benefit of a new and wider audience in the future.

With the approval of his family, friends, and several of his colleagues, I undertook the task of selecting 70 representative essays for this anthology from among the many Dr. Massey had written for the Journal. For ease of reading, I arranged them into sections by topics e.g., aging, ethics, patient care, education, and technology. Throughout these essays, Dr. Massey frequently refers to his favorite physicians, authors, and "heroes"—William Osler, Thomas Browne, Albert Schweitzer, T.S. Eliot, Montaigne, Mark Twain, Lewis Thomas, and others. It therefore seemed appropriate to turn to these "friends" and "companions" of his for a few words to introduce each of the sections of this book. The quotations chosen would, I suspect, have brought a smile to his face.

As medical students read these essays and discuss them with their peers, they will find much to reflect upon—ethical issues, moral values, patient care, and the historical background of their chosen profession. Physicians currently immersed in the hectic world of an active medical practice, with perhaps far too few opportunities for reading and contemplation, will discover within these short articles and literary vignettes timely and digestible nuggets of information and common sense. And for those who are in the final stages of their medical careers, or who have already laid aside stethoscopes, scalpels, and other tools of their profession, these essays may provide an opportunity to look back upon their years of practice with satisfaction and say—yes, I too was once part of that wonderful world of medicine.

For these essays remind us all that those who choose to and are allowed to care for their fellow human beings are, as Bob Massey wrote (p. 12), "privileged to serve in a glorious profession."

Martin Duke, MD

REFERENCE

1. O'Leary R: Joseph Garland, M.D., 1893–1973. The Writer. *N Engl J Med* 1973; 289(12):640–1.

Section 1—Medical Education

Education without values, as useful as it is, seems rather to make a man a more clever devil.

C.S. Lewis (1898–1963)

To study the phenomenon of disease without books is to sail an uncharted sea, while to study books without patients is not to go to sea at all.

William Osler (1849–1919)

The Role of Medical Educators

THIS fall the future doctors for more than 10 million Americans have entered the nation's 112 medical schools to begin a period of education, training, and acculturation which will consume over 10 percent of their allotted lifespan and which will, in almost every instance, effect a change in their lives akin to a religious conversion.

Medical education means distilling out of a confusing mass of old and new biological knowledge those facts and relationships which are judged important to the understanding and practice of medicine. The tidal wave of the Renaissance which began in Italy 600 years ago and which struck biology over 100 years ago may be nearing its crest in the life sciences in this final quarter of the 20th century. In the midst of the high excitement accompanying such intensity of intellectual activity, it is difficult, perhaps impossible, to tease out and present the "core" of knowledge which the student ought somehow to master. It may be quite unimportant. It may be enough that the students sense the excitement. Undoubtedly, some will find that they can never again live without it.

Medical education means teaching many new skills and reinforcing others already learned. Recently, Horn and others,[1] reviewing recent work on the neural mechanisms involved in learning, have shown fairly conclusively that learning is accompanied in the developing nervous system by biochemical and morphological changes in specific portions of the brain. Whether the potential for similar plasticity exists also in the adult mammalian brain is less clear; as educators, our faith is that it must! The skills of observing, sensing, relating, comparing, and concluding must be brought to a level of excellence quite the same as that expected of a highly trained airplane pilot. Human lives are dependent on those skills in both instances.

Medical education means reinforcing some attitudes, modifying others, and, perhaps in some instances, challenging and fundamentally changing some of those that relate to the major taboos of our culture.[2] The qualities which we have in mind when we imagine the ideal physician are, by and large, ethical and behavioral qualities. Some will object that such an image, if composed only of these qualities, might be nothing more than that of the well-meaning bungler. If by ethical qualities appropriate to a physician the objectors have in mind personal honesty and a vague feeling of wanting to help suffering humanity, I must emphatically agree with them. The warm and loving feeling of wanting to help must be stiffened by an imperative of concern which may, at times, depend not at all on feelings; and personal honesty must be transformed into an intellectual integrity and curiosity by which the student, and later the physician, recognizes the continuing and accurate acquisition of knowledge and the improvement of skills as imperatives incumbent upon himself first, but also upon others in his profession.

Medical education is an initiation into a new culture. José Ortega y Gasset, the great Spanish humanist and historian, wrote that "the collective life of a people, a nation, is an intimate—and to a certain extent a secret—matter, very like what those words mean when one says of a personal life that it is an intimacy within itself, and no one who looks at it from the outside can easily come to understand it."[3] Medicine, the profession, the institution, the culture, is like that. Its ideals, its heroes, its traditions and ceremonies sustain its members in their physical, emotional, ethical, and intellectual exertions. The student must be absorbed into this world of medicine; he must come to look at it from the inside and, in a certain sense, at all of life through its windows. As educators we must sense the times when it is good to bring forth the sagas and to celebrate our art and its science.

REFERENCES

1. Horn G, Rose SPR, Bateson PPG: Experience and plasticity in the central nervous system. *Science* 1973 August 10; 181(4099):506–14.
2. Knight JA: *Medical Student: Doctor in the Making*. New York: Appleton-Century-Crofts; 1973.
3. Ortega y Gasset J: *An Interpretation of Universal History.* Translated by Mildred Adams. New York: WW Norton; 1973.

Connecticut Medicine 1973; 37(10):516

American Medical Education: No One Does It Better

TO the question, "When did modern medical education begin in America," the answer might be, "1893, a century ago, when Johns Hopkins admitted its first class." At least the pattern was visible then: selective admissions after a bachelor's degree, coeducation, two years of laboratory science, two years of learning by "doing" on clinical services, postgraduate hospital work—all much the way it is now. With a few exceptions, a century later America's 126 medical schools, following Abraham Flexner's idea of medical education, adhere to the pattern, and are more alike than different.

Since 1979 the University of Connecticut School of Medicine has accepted a small number of European medical students each year to spend from three to nine months in research or clinical work. Many other medical schools in the United States do the same; several hundred students from Germany spend part of their clinical years in an American school. Nearly half of these men and women later enter academic medicine in Germany. A recent report by one of them (her research thesis) noted that almost all believe that American clinical education is superior to theirs at home, that clinical teachers here treat them as colleagues, love to teach, and are remarkably generous with their time.

The visiting students form lasting friendships with American students, and are impressed with how hard they work and how determined they are to master every detail of their clinical work. They believe some are less well prepared in the basic sciences. They are not surprised that few speak German, or any foreign language, but find it curious that not many have an interest in current events, history, literature, art, and music.

Though our faculties never tire of reworking the curriculum, medical education in the United States and Canada is quite simply the best in the world. The problem is with our first 16 years of general education.

We have history majors who are unsure about why or when the Western or Eastern Roman Empires declined and fell; they are uncertain about the decade of the American Civil War! American medical students rarely know who William Osler was, but German students do, although they know more about Rudolf Virchow. Most German students have had Greek, Latin, and speak English and French fluently. A few have even read F. Scott Fitzgerald novels, and most know *Tom Sawyer.* Of course they know Goethe and Schiller, but they know a fair amount of Shakespeare, too. They have missed the liberating benefits of a one-millimeter-deep multicultural education; their view of the world is, as a consequence, hopelessly Eurocentric. They have apparently been spared the blessings of postmodernism; at least they know Western Civ in depth.

As I review the transcripts of medical school applicants, I rarely discern a coherent course of study. Two years of a foreign language, now forgotten, a scattering of "humanities," courses on gender or race in society, a survey of Indian philosophy for those who could not distinguish Plato from Aristotle from William James, and one semester of the American novel, modern dance, or marketing. Sciences, most of which are repeated in medical school, pile up in the fourth year because, as one dean said, they know how to make A's in them.

None of this may matter. Most medical students become competent, caring physicians; some, world-class biomedical scientists. They come from families where important values of truth-telling, service, common sense, and self-discipline have been taught and lived. They needed some years to grow up in, and, despite the academic frivolity that few took seriously, they managed. When I try to make sense of these transcripts with their incoherent, even silly, lists of courses, I am saddened that hard-working parents spend thousands for this "college education." Sunk as we are in the Western rationalist tradition, medical school faculties might offer better liberal arts curriculum, beginning with Latin and medical history, and exchanging Celsus for Caesar! We could come up with a great list of novels and short stories for the clinical years.

Connecticut Medicine 1993; 57(12):829

Thumbs Up, Thumbs Down

APPLICATIONS for the medical school class of '86 have started to arrive, and admissions committees will shortly begin their task of choosing those men and women who will serve medicine from 1990 until they retire in the '20s and '30s of the next century.

Medical College Admission Test (MCAT) scores, grade point averages, extracurricular activities, letters of recommendation, and the interviews—which are the best predictors and how should they be used to pick our next generation of physicians? An A in organic chemistry may be the best assurance of academic success in the basic sciences. Our experience has suggested that the interview, viewed retrospectively, predicts outstanding success or failure in the clinical years; that may run counter to the experience of others.

Admissions committee members could, I suppose, make up a description of the ideal medical student and agree upon most of the desirable qualities, but I suspect the final picture would be a hodge-podge, with contradictory traits that could not possibly exist together in the same person. The committee would doubtlessly fall again into confusion if asked to consider whether ideal medical students and ideal doctors possess the same qualities of heart and mind.

The old instruments have lost their sharp edges. Grades are inflated in most colleges, although this is often denied; because there are no grades higher than A, the good and the best are indistinguishable. Students may for a price prepare themselves for the MCAT, and cynics say that whether students are prepared or not, all that is measured is their skill in taking computer-scored examinations. Every college wants a high number of its students who apply to professional schools to gain admittance. As competition for students becomes keener, this want will become more insistent. Letters of recommendation are useful only if the code words are known.

Even if we could know more, would we know what we wanted? Intelligence, certainly, but what kind? Should it be the intelligence of a Mozart, an Einstein, or a Schweitzer? Osler discounted his own intellectual endowment and said that whatever success he had achieved had been owing to hard work. We should like to know of our applicants how they have lived and what they have thought. We don't speak much of constitutional types anymore, lacking the data, but we secretly believe that there are types of people—types of faces, types of bodies, types of voices—some of which we favor over others. That belief may urge us on to confess that some characteristics tell us more than what we ought reasonably to inhere in them. There are some types we intuitively trust more than others, and some we would positively distrust. As scientists and egalitarians we worry about these notions; we suspect that they are unscientific and we are ashamed of their illiberality.

Novelists do not have these scruples. They know about constitutional differences; that is why they take such pains to describe people, how far apart their eyes are and how weak their chins, or how soft and flabby their hands. In fact, they may still use the old humoral terms which served medicine from the time of Hippocrates until a century ago: phlegmatic, sanguine, melancholic, choleric. We have added others to these of the ancient humoralists: nervous, introverted, neurasthenic, passive-aggressive, schizoid, depressive. Exponents of the ancient four would see in these only variations on the theme. Shakespeare knew the system [*Julius Caesar*]:

> Let me have men about me that are fat;
> Sleek-headed men, and such as sleep o'nights.
> Yond' Cassius has a lean and hungry look;
> He thinks too much: such men are dangerous.

Cassius was a melancholic, and therefore to be feared, so Caesar said; there was more loyalty in someone phlegmatic, more pleasure in someone sanguine.

It would be simpler if admissions committees could type their applicants; if somehow in the short space of an hour, they could make out the depth of moral commitment, the love of mankind, the intelligence, the sensitivity, the common sense, the physical stamina, and the ethical toughness of an aspirant to the priesthood of Aesculapius. Perhaps a Shakespeare, or a Dickens, or a George Eliot on the committee would help, but failing that, doctors will have to decide when doctors disagree, or else get help from fellow academicians in other disciplines, and from lawyers, clergymen, patients, legislators, and business people.

Unless we are prepared to allow one good humored person the omniscience needed to make these choices, next year's class will be picked by a committee whose members will not have lost all traces of the doctrine of the four humors, who will be looking beyond the MCAT scores for signs of acuity and hints of the cardinal virtues.

Connecticut Medicine 1981; 45(9):607

Marketable Skills or an Education?

IN a recent University of Connecticut convocation held to honor former President Homer D. Babbidge, President DiBiaggio spoke of challenges for the future of university education: "Perhaps one of the most serious is the growing predisposition of our entering students to focus on specific job or career preparation." He went on to affirm "—the certain knowledge that no one's long-term interest is best served by this approach—not society's, not employers', and most importantly to us, not the student's."

This is the ancient faith of the teacher; today the light of that faith is burning low, and some, despairing of making converts and weary from seeking for any who will even listen, have gone over to the other side, to the side of the trainers. There are so many gadgets to learn about in a technological civilization, so many skills to acquire, so many competitors to out-guess and out-maneuver, so much money to be made that taking time for an education is an unaffordable luxury, even supposing it had any special appeal. When you think of it, the appeal of learning may be little more than a seduction to a kind of self-indulgence, quite out of place in the world of technology, corporate structures, and electronic games.

The old faith, however, refuses to die; it has been around long enough to be part of us, and at other times when the number of its disciples have been reduced to a remnant, society has found ways of protecting them. There have always been academies, libraries, monasteries, universities and large and small citadels of learning preserved by society to assure its salvation, or at least its respectability.

In medical education we have fallen into the habit of imagining the future and then trying to design educational programs that "will prepare our students for medical practice in the 21st century." We all think and talk that way at times, but that turns quickly into a kind of "specific job or career preparation" that President DiBiaggio referred to. Even if we were to be successful in accommodating our courses of study to the biological revolution, the explosion in technology, the aging of our population, the excessive numbers of physicians, the prospective payment systems, and the commercialization of medicine, the enterprise would not work. Beyond five to seven years the future is not knowable and any description of it is almost certain to be wrong. The future is more than the way things will be; it is also the values we shall come to attach to them. That makes for an impossible set of variables, shaky ground upon which to build an education or even to design part of a curriculum. It is enough to learn something about the present and the past that has led up to it; enough to get an education in the liberal arts and sciences, and to learn one or two things well; enough for the medical student to learn human biology and the methods of clinical medicine and to learn them very well. For better or worse, the future will most certainly take care of itself; how well it does will depend a little on how we manage the present and understand the past, but more on matters which now we only "see through a glass darkly."

What then should we be telling our students about medicine? Everything, of course, but especially we should tell them to pay more attention to their patients and less to themselves; we should not be ashamed to tell them that medicine is first of all a moral vocation with a call to perfection and that it is a special privilege to have received that call, never mind from where; we should remind them that medicine is more than technology, although that is part of it, more than science although it depends upon it, and that it is never a business, although right now almost everyone is trying to make it into one. Tell them never to call it the health-care industry and never to speak of profitability or their market share; if they have been liberally educated they will understand the power embedded in words like those. Words like vocation, obligation, duty, commitment, respect, compassion, and selflessness have even more power, but they need to be spoken first and mentioned often without embarrassment. They recur over and over in the course of a liberal education; they are the serious soul of liberal learning, saving it from mere pedantry and luxurious self-indulgence and making it the best kind of baggage to carry into the future.

Connecticut Medicine 1984; 48(4):267

L'Allegro

LARGE meetings of physicians and medical educators are rarely abundantly cheerful affairs; the recent meeting of the Association of American Medical Colleges was no exception. One of the speakers, not a physician, showed a slide of a down-in-the-mouth, low-spirited face surmounting a bow tie: "This is a physician, 1987 (or 1972, or 1965)," he said. We recognized ourselves!

Most of the talk during the meeting was of the declining numbers of applicants to medical school, the putative physician surplus, inadequate research support, excessive medical school dependence on patient-care income, cost containment, competition, and the effect of all these vexing conditions on medical education and patient care. Of course, most speakers gravely asserted that these were all challenges, and that should mean opportunity, and that the worst of times could be turned into the best of times; a few even denied that there were problems serious enough to require elaborate solutions.

William Osler had written in his essay, "The Student Life," a farewell address to Canadian and American medical students, in 1905:

> Hilarity and good humour, a breezy cheerfulness, a 'nature sloping toward the southern side,' as Lowell has it, help enormously both in the study and the practice of medicine. To many of a sombre and sour disposition it is hard to maintain good spirits amid the trials and tribulations of the day, and yet it is an unpardonable mistake to go about among patients with a long face.

It was the economist, Uwe Reinhardt, who at the AAMC meeting was gently chiding physicians for their long faces. He said that many of his doctor friends have declared that they would never want *their* children to enter medicine. "Fine," was his answer, "then there'll be more room for mine." He went on to remind us that ours was a glorious profession, something which most of us know but rarely tell anyone about. In spite of all our complaining about the ponderous bureaucracy, unsympathetic politicians, ungrateful patients, and mean-spirited lawyers, we have rarely met a colleague who was not overjoyed when a son or daughter switched from a major in history, signed up for organic chemistry, and applied to medical school.

In his recent excellent book, *The Discovery of Insulin*, Michael Bliss[1] has written a moving account of the transformation in young diabetics when insulin was first used in their treatment. These patients are described in a chapter called "Resurrection"; they had indeed returned from what would have been certain death, either from starvation or keto-acidosis, to a fully restored life. One of them, Elizabeth Hughes, daughter of Charles Evans Hughes, was 15 years old, five feet tall, and weighed 45 pounds when she first received insulin; she had already exceeded her life expectancy, thanks to the starvation diet imposed by her physician, Frederick Allen, immediately after her disease had been diagnosed in 1918. Just before Frederick Banting began giving her insulin in Toronto in August 1922, she had been on a 300-calorie diet; within five weeks she was eating 2,700 calories, her urine was almost sugar-free, and she had gained 10 pounds; she continued gaining two to three pounds a week. Three months later, no longer an invalid, she returned home to Washington. Elizabeth Hughes subsequently graduated from Barnard, married, and raised her three children. Almost 60 years later, after some 45,000 injections of insulin, not only was she well, but her vision was good. She died suddenly in 1981, aged 74, following a heart attack.

> Hence, loathed Melancholy,
> Of Cerberus and blackest Midnight born.
>
> John Milton, *L'Allegro*

It takes an economist and an historian to remind us: we are privileged to serve in a glorious profession.

REFERENCE

1. Bliss M: *The Discovery of Insulin.* Chicago: University of Chicago Press; 1982:304.

Connecticut Medicine 1987; 51(12):821

Quite Random Notes to a Young Doctor

MY grandson Jonathan has just begun his first postgraduate year at Georgetown after his graduation this spring from Vanderbilt Medical School. We have seen little of one another over the years, but have kept in touch mostly by mail at Christmas and birthdays. Now, as he enters our ancient profession as a *Medicinae Doctor verus,* I feel driven to share some grandfatherly observations, many from a time long gone and a culture that survives mostly as history.

Twenty years ago, near the beginnings of the corporate take-over of our profession by the moneyed crowd, Paul Starr published his now largely forgotten social history of American medicine, warning against the coming disaster:

> The failure to rationalize medical services under public control meant that sooner or later they would be rationalized under private control. Instead of public regulation there will be private regulation, and instead of public planning there will be corporate planning. Instead of public financing for prepaid plans . . . there will be corporate financing for private plans . . . whose interests will be determined by the rate of return on investments. That is the future toward which American medicine now seems to be heading.[1]

Corporate, investor-driven medicine has come of age and, though there remain some pockets of sanity, the social and political will to change seems remarkably feeble. I shall write about these matters to my grandson, trying to enlist him in the resistance movement, but he surely has more pressing matters at this beginning of his professional life. It is better that I repeat some of the words that tell of our profession's ancient wisdom and nobility.

I will send him a copy of the Hippocratic Oath—not the debased and politically correct oath used today, if used at all, in commencement ceremonies. Sherwin Nuland once wrote of Hippocrates:

> A culture that sets its moral course by the Ten Commandments is thus at one with a culture that lives by the words of the Father of Medicine:
>
> *With purity and with holiness I will pass my life and practice my Art.*[2]

Jon has owned a copy of Dr. Nuland's book, *Doctors,* for several years; I will urge him to read again this first chapter, "The Totem of Medicine."

The 19th-century physician, Hermann Nothnagel, had been inspired by German classicism, humanism, and especially by the work of Immanuel Kant. In his inaugural lecture in 1882 at the Vienna Medical School he declared, echoing Hippocrates, "Only a good man can be a great physician."

My professor of medicine, Gordon Myers, introduced me to Francis W. Peabody's *Doctor and Patient* in 1945, and another good friend made me a gift of his 1930 first-edition copy. The last few lines of the second essay, "The Care of the Patient," have, using Osler's words, "hit and struck and helped:"

> The good physician knows his patients through and through, and his knowledge is bought dearly. Time, sympathy and understanding must be lavishly dispensed, but the reward is to be found in that personal bond which forms the greatest satisfaction of the practice of medicine.
>
> One of the essential qualities of the clinician is interest in humanity, for the secret of the care of the patient is in caring for the patient.[3]

In his fourth and last essay in *Doctor and Patient,* Peabody concludes by striking a clear chord for our times: "What we want is less of the system and law that kills and more of the spirit that gives life."[3]

And, of course, I shall remind him of William Osler. Jonathan owns both the Cushing and the Bliss biographies, but medical school allows scant time for reading, and, since his generation knows almost nothing of any history before the 1960s, these impressive volumes will seem to speak of things from another world. I suppose one of the most well-known of the Oslerian aphorisms comes from his "Address Delivered to Yale Students, Sunday Evening, April 20th, 1913."[4]

> . . . I picked up a volume of Carlyle, and on the page I opened there was the familiar sentence—*Our main business is not to see what lies dimly at a distance, but to do what lies clearly at hand.*

He urged that life be lived in "day-tight compartments":

> The load of to-morrow, added to that of yesterday, carried to-day makes the strongest falter. Shut off the future as tightly as the past. . . . The future is to-day—there is no to-morrow.

A medical student in this early 21st century has undoubtedly learned by rote the mantra of contemporary bioethics: autonomy, nonmaleficence, beneficence, and justice. Admirable as these midlevel principles are there is little here to feed the spirit: let the patient decide, don't do bad things, do good things, be even-handed and fair. A stronger frame is formed from the Aristotelian virtues of courage, temperance, liberality, good temper, prudence, wisdom, and justice, and the Pauline graces of faith, hope, and love.

The good doctor should help the patient decide after she has heard and understood her choices, their costs and their consequences, as well as the reasons for his professional opinion. All this should flow naturally from their trusting relationship as friends. This takes time. I once heard a lawyer tell medical students at Yale to "make friends with your patients; friends don't sue friends!" That is one reason but not reason enough. Francis Peabody reminds us that the personal bond between patient and physician is what makes the practice of medicine the amazing joy that it is.

I recently talked of these things to a group of primary-care residents. One spoke up: "Doctor, that's all very nice, but it's impossible. In a 15-minute encounter we don't have time for all that!"

Finally, I will remind Jonathan that at least a half hour, better an hour, at bedtime, be spent with radio and television silent, the journals laid aside, and a good book in hand. Many of us who are still around from the first half of the last century will recall our graduation gift from Eli Lilly and Company, *Aequanimitas,* by Sir William Osler, Bt., MD, FRS. We all knew about Osler; we had studied from his *Principles and Practice of Medicine.* Several of our teachers' teachers had learned their medicine first-hand from Osler, and my chief during my residency years had been one of Dr. Osler's clinical clerks. It was rumored that he kept a signed photo of the great doctor in his bedroom and genuflected before it morning and night! Giants and saints walked in the smaller medical world of those years, and we took them all seriously.

Osler, who had never earned a BA degree, recommended, at the very end of *Aequanimitas,* a bedside library that now after nearly 100 years has a distinct Victorian-Edwardian fragrance. It would help us acquire, he wrote, "the education, if not of a scholar, at least of a gentleman." I would still include, as he did, the Bible and Shakespeare as the first two on the list, and perhaps Montaigne and Cervantes. Harold Bloom's *The Western Canon* is a good guide for building a collection. Some wisdom is to be found this way, and joy, and peace; such things are rare in our postmodern world of ethical relativism and money-driven medical care.

REFERENCES

1. Starr P: *The Social Transformation of American Medicine.* New York: Basic Books, Inc.; 1982:449.
2. Nuland SB: *Doctors: The Biography of Medicine.* New York: Alfred A. Knopf; 1988:29.

3. Peabody FW: *Doctor and Patient.* New York: The Macmillan Company; 1930.
4. Osler W: *A Way of Life.* Springfield, IL: Charles C. Thomas; 1969.

Connecticut Medicine 2002; 66(7):435–6

Section 2—Medical Care and the Art of Medicine

The truth of the matter is that the practice of medicine is intensely personal and no system or machine can be substituted for the personal relationship.

Francis W. Peabody (1881–1927)

Wherever the art of medicine is loved, there is also a love of humanity.

Hippocrates (c. 460–377 B.C.)

Down-sizing Time: Efficient but Hardly Effective

> A doctor who cannot take a good history and a patient who cannot give one are in danger of giving and receiving bad treatment.
>
> *Paul Dudley White (1886–1973)*

IN their greed for profit our managed-care masters, most of whom know little or nothing about medicine, are so bent on managing time that each patient visit is but a brief encounter. "I saw the doctor for only about eight minutes," my neighbor told me, and asked, after attributing this irritating visit to managed care, "Why aren't you doctors fighting back?"

The business crowd who have moved in on the practice of medicine cannot be blamed for doing what they have been trained to do; they know, until they get sick themselves, that the purpose of medicine is to make money.

They know also that standards for diagnosis and treatment can be written, are being written, and can be made into computer programs so that with a few key strokes the physician can generate a diagnosis from which a treatment plan will be printed out. They betray their ignorance of human nature and history by being quite certain that preventive medicine will make expensive diagnosis and treatment rarely necessary. "Can't 85% of all diseases be prevented? That's what I've read. Why don't you doctors get on with it?" Anyway, prevention could be ladled out by a string of low-paid health-care workers, social workers, nutritionists, exercise therapists, acupuncturists, naturopaths, group therapists, counselors, sex therapists, and spiritual gurus. None of this will make a dent in the costs of "the health-care industry," but will vastly expand profit margins and market share.

Years ago, a brilliant clinical scientist, having listened to as much prevention talk as he could stand, commented, "Wear seat belts, don't get fat, don't smoke, have one or two drinks a day, no more, walk up two flights, down three, and get your flu shot. What else is there?" The receptionist, while taking your blood pressure, could tell you all that in less than eight minutes, and maybe pass out a tract on safe condom use or low-fat chocolate bars, or even low-fat fat.

William Mayo is reported to have said that ". . . the ideal of medicine is to eliminate the need of a physician." This was Dr. Will's sentiment as an after-dinner speaker; as a surgeon he knew better. Preventing disease has, for the most part, been a by-product of the industrial revolution, aseptic surgery, and the science of immunology. Even internists know that a world without surgeons would be a scary place indeed. We could stop worrying about population growth! And, by the way, AIDS is one of the most preventable diseases around and yet it is the major killer of young people, especially young men, and, world-wide, continues to roar right along.

It is time, more than anything else, that remains the essential element in the care of the sick and the worried well, and time it is that the management wizards want to "down-size." Even in medical schools students are taught to take a focused history, not a complete history, perform a focused physical examination, and never mind asking about those things that matter to the patient, their jobs, their worries, their families, the world series, and the next election. The students' questions become stereotyped, and their manner patronizing as they ask a total stranger without looking up from the chart, "Well, Mary, what brings us to the clinic today?" After all, time is money, and Mrs. Mary Jones must be out and on her way to the lab in 10 minutes. No time to learn much about Mary. Teach them how it will be in the real world, not how to change the world.

A professor of medicine told his house staff: "Take your time. Histories take time to unfold, and when they do, you're 90% along the way to a diagnosis and a plan." Another, a Regius Professor, said, "Let the disease declare itself if it's not obviously an emergency. You may not even need the lab!" Look again at Sir Zachary Cope's plan for the early diagnosis of the acute abdomen. An eight minute visit?

How much time is needed to feel and express sympathy, empathy, and begin to care for the patient and show it? How long to build a friendship and to be responsible *for* the patient rather than *to* your friendly nurturing HMO?

Managed care, that is, care managed for profit, will, we pray, be a short footnote in medical history. If we don't bring it down, surely our patients will.

Connecticut Medicine 1995; 59(12):749

Man Has an Inborn Craving for Medicine

William Osler (1849–1919)

THIS past month we may have felt the ground trembling beneath our feet. First the revelation that the antidepressants, selective serotonin reuptake inhibitors (SSRIs), were not dramatically more effective than placebos, and might occasionally be associated with suicidal impulses—hardly surprising in depressed patients. Then came a study showing that arthroscopic knee surgery, when used in the treatment of osteoarthritis, may be about as effective as a sham operation. And finally the revelation that ovarian hormone therapy for menopausal symptoms increased the risk of breast and ovarian cancer, strokes, and heart attacks—although here the figures were hardly dramatic, and most of us had assumed all this was so anyway.

The history of medicine is full of procedures and remedies that have been useless, or even harmful, but which had doctors and patients fooled for years. In fact, wiser physicians among us have known that most of the ills that plague us will get better by themselves. William Osler was called a therapeutic nihilist, though nihilist may be too strong a term.

In his 1892 textbook, Osler recommended bleeding in cases of hypertension associated with congestive failure, in some cases of cerebral hemorrhage, sometimes in pneumonia, in emphysema if patients were dyspneic and livid, and even in sunstroke! He wrote:

> During the first five decades of this century the profession bled too much, but during the last decades we have certainly bled too little. Pneumonia is one of the diseases in which a timely venesection may save life. In a full-blooded healthy man with a high fever and bounding pulse the abstraction of from twenty to thirty ounces of blood is in every way beneficial. . . .[1]

This advice, though with a hesitating touch "small amounts are sufficient," still appeared in my 15th (1944) edition of the Osler textbook edited by Henry Christian.[2]

Some Oslerian wisdom about humanity's love affair with pills includes:

> A desire to take medicine is, perhaps, the great feature which distinguishes us from other animals.
>
> One of the first duties of the physician is to educate the masses not to take medicine.

> One should treat as many patients as possible with a new drug while it still has the power to heal.
>
> I suppose, as a body, clergymen are better educated than any other, yet they are notorious supporters of all the nostrums and humbuggery . . .; and I find that the further away from the decrees of the Council of Trent, the more apt they are to be steeped in thaumaturgic and Galenical superstition.

William Bean wrote that Osler "freely prescribed alcohol as a stimulant for the aged, including his mother. According to George Washington Stephens' family, his preference was for gin."[3]

And from another physician, Oliver Wendell Holmes:

> No families take so little medicine as those of doctors, except those of apothecaries.
>
> Throw out opium, which the Creator himself seems to prescribe, . . . throw out wine, which is a food, and the vapors which produce the miracle of anesthesia, and I firmly believe that if the whole materia medica, *as now used*, could be sunk to the bottom of the sea, it would be all the better for mankind—and all the worse for the fishes.

My professor of pharmacology, Fritz Yonkman, urged us—this was in the mid 1940s—to learn 10 drugs well, we would rarely need more! Well, there have been some impressively valuable new ones since then, but perhaps not as many as the massive pharmaceutical industry would have us believe. As I recall, the *Physicians' Desk Reference* in the 1950s was less than three quarters of an inch thick; it is now more than four times that, about 4,000 pages. Recently a pharmaceutical firm executive said the industry had at least 800 new drugs in the pipeline, 300 aimed at the Medicare crowd!

Antidepressants now represent, according to psychopharmacologist David Healy, a 10 billion dollar market. Healy further asserts that as much as 50% of the therapeutic literature is ghost-written. He writes that we are "now apparently in an Age of Depression." The antidepressant market grew some 800% during the 1990s. His publications on the risks of the SSRIs, as well as their somewhat questionable effectiveness, led him into legal difficulties and resulted in a major university rescinding a job offer it had made to him.[4]

Last month the Hartford *Courant* reported that "spending on prescription drugs is growing faster than any other area of health care, yet pharmaceutical manufacturers act is if there is no problem." Their approval ratings have fallen 20% in the past five years, almost as much as HMOs! And there is a shortage of pharmacists!

None of this should come as a surprise. Congress is talking about relieving the burden on the elderly by providing a prescription drug benefit, but the major benefit, by increasing sales, will go to the pharmaceutical manufacturers, having been paid for by taxpayers. By itself, a costly Medicare drug benefit program will hardly solve the problem for either the individual or the nation.

With an occasional exception, doctors should prescribe generic drugs. Rarely has the overwhelming advantage of a new "me-too" drug been proven in ethical, disinterested clinical trials. And, in cases of depression, we should recognize, not a diagnosable disease, but a very common symptom to which all flesh is heir. Sometimes it may be far more than that, and SSRIs are available generically, as well as other even more effective treatments.

> Despite long-standing critiques of the conduct of underpowered clinical trials, the practice not only remains widespread, but also has garnered increasing support.[5]

Newspaper, magazine, and television advertising of pharmaceuticals should become as much a "no, no" as cigarette and liquor advertising. It may be nearly as harmful! Last month the *Courant* carried a one and one-third page advertisement for Remicade (25 July). I watch little television, but when the tube is on, a drug commercial is sure to appear within 10 minutes, urging patients to appeal to their physicians to prescribe some new miracle potion, which includes in its inflated price the expense of misleading advertising and the salaries of thousands of detail-men.

Until relatively recently, medical schools and drug companies were rarely linked in their research efforts. Research grants from the NIH sustained most of the faculty's research programs. Derek Bok, former president of Harvard University, "... never stopped worrying that the desire of a medical school or university to increase profits would conflict with its academic mission. . . . It will take very strong leadership to keep the profit motive from gradually eroding the values on which the welfare and reputation of universities ultimately depend."[6]

The solution to all this escapes me, but a Medicare benefit for drugs of questionable benefit will surely not solve the problem. The beginning of a cure lies, as it usually does, with physicians; they must learn to comfort and reassure more, to test and prescribe less. Lewis Thomas, referring to the use of medical care by doctors' families, wrote:

> If my hunch, based on the small sample of professional friends is correct, these people appear to use modern medicine quite differently from the ways in which we have systematically been educating the public over the last few decades. . . . Doctors' families do tend to complain that they receive less medical attention than their friends and neighbors, but they

> seem a normal, generally healthy lot, with a remarkably low incidence of iatrogenic illness.
>
> The great secret known to internists and learned early in marriage by internists' wives, but still hidden from the general public, is that most things get better by themselves. Most things, in fact, are better by morning.[7]

He also reminded us that much of our research efforts are toward half-way technologies, of limited value and terribly expensive. We should be seeking instead the high technology that "comes as the result of genuine understanding of the disease mechanisms, and when it becomes available, relatively inexpensive, relatively simple, and relatively easy to deliver."

The whole thing about the high cost of new, questionably useful drugs seems to parallel the recently exuberant stock market; it is all about money and greed. A highly respected hospital administrator, now retired, once commented to his board, "When the talk comes to money, all other values fly out the window!"

Perhaps history will take care of our expensive love affair with pills as it has the overvalued stock market. History, often with some imaginative help, usually does.

REFERENCES

1. Osler W: *The Principles and Practice of Medicine*. New York: Appleton and Company; 1892:530.
2. Christian HA: *The Principles and Practice of Medicine*, 15th ed. New York and London: D. Appleton-Century Company, Inc.; 1944:65.
3. Bliss M: *William Osler: A Life in Medicine.* New York: Oxford University Press; 1999:108.
4. Healy D: Conflicting interests in Toronto: Anatomy of a controversy at the interface of academia and industry. *Perspect Biol Med* 2002; 45:250–63,
5. Halpern SD, Karlawish JHT, Berlin JA: The continuing unethical conduct of underpowered clinical trials. *JAMA* 2002; 288:358–65.
6. Ludmerer KM: *Time to Heal: American Medical Education from the Turn of the Century to the Era of Managed Care*. New York: Oxford University Press; 1999:342.
7. Thomas L: *The Lives of a Cell: Notes of a Biology Watcher.* New York: Viking Press; 1974:85.

Connecticut Medicine 2002; 66(8):495–6

So Little Time

A YOUNG internist told me recently that unless he saw 25 to 30 patients in his office each day he could not pay his expenses and make a reasonable income for his family. I calculated that he must spend no more than 10 to 15 minutes with each patient.

I recall working that fast when I took sick call during my army days, but my patients were mostly young, healthy males with straight-forward complaints; 10 minutes was usually enough, and if aspirin or reassurance failed, they would be back the next day. For the worried, middle-aged patient, the depressed 80-year-old, the anxious teenager, a 10-minute visit must seem like a very long run for a short slide.

Several months ago a patient whom I had not seen in 25 years called from New Mexico just to say "hello." I knew better, so we talked for 30 or 40 minutes, trying to get around to what she really was calling about. Since I had last seen her she had been partially disabled by what she understood to be cerebellar degeneration; her neurologist said he could do nothing for her and her internist passed off her increasing abdominal discomfort and bowel symptoms as part of the disease. When we finished the long-distance phone call she said that just talking had made her feel better, and would I mind if she called again sometime? No one had listened much to her, she said, especially since she was now 70 years old and in a wheel chair.

Fortunately I was able to do more than just listen, although that was what had been important to her; I arranged an appointment at the Mayo Clinic, which is where she felt secure in going. Later through telephone calls and letters from the Clinic I learned that she had had a partial resection and colostomy, and now seemed to be doing well.

After she returned home she called to thank me and to say that she now has two places to call when she needs to talk about her medical problems—Connecticut and Minnesota!

Homeopathy was one of the most successful of the 19th-century medical sects, and it appealed especially to the better educated urban upper classes. Part of its attraction almost certainly lay in its avoidance of purging and bleeding but more was in the care with which homeopathic physicians elicited their clinical histories. Since the choice of the diluted drugs to be used in treatment depended entirely upon the patient's symptoms, successful therapy rested upon a painstaking review of the clinical history. That took time, and time to spend talking with the doctor was what most patients wanted and needed.

The homeopathic armamentarium of drugs had little pharmacologic effect; today's stimulants and depressants, more widely used by far than the "morbific agents" in Samuel Hahnemann's *Organon* [5th Ed. 1833], have baneful effects if improperly prescribed; an accurate history is essential to avoid doing more harm than good. Of equal importance, it takes time for friendship and trust to grow. A wise lawyer once reminded our medical students, "Good friends don't sue friends." More important, mutual respect and trust are the very substance of the patient-doctor relationship that we talk so much about but so often fail to have time for; how could we when we must measure out time with coffee spoons?

More and more patients see hospitals as big businesses and doctors as entrepreneurs; big business, behaving efficiently, nearly always becomes bureaucratic, impersonal, and unpleasant. The "health-care organization" almost certainly will have put the patient in her place by the time she gets to the physician. His first work is to undo the mounting anger and fear, to listen, to reassure, to build trust, to persuade the patient that, contrary to all her impressions, their relationship will be professional, not commercial.

I recall a fine clinical teacher assuring a medical student that he should not worry that he had not gotten a satisfactory story of his patient's illness during his hour-long interview; "Come back tomorrow; the patient will know you better, and, anyway, most clinical histories take time to develop." No worthwhile story is ever told in a hurry.

Connecticut Medicine 1988; 52(10):627

Too Much Science?

YOU may recall that in the opening paragraph of his essay, "The Care of the Patient," Francis Peabody wrote:

> The most common criticism made at present by older practitioners is that young graduates have been taught a great deal about the mechanism of disease, but very little about the practice of medicine—or, to put it more bluntly, they are too "scientific" and do not know how to take care of patients.[1]

Last year, 60 years later, Samuel Thier spoke of the criticism aimed at house officers and medical students that they were inhumane and excessively scientific, and then added, "When you stop hearing that new graduates are too scientific, it means the field is not advancing and training them better than the old. . . ."[2]

Both Peabody and Thier were trying to say that medicine should not be either all science or all humanism (although Peabody did not use that term), nor, I believe, were they implying that it was a little of each. In 1927 scientific medicine was still a novelty for many doctors over 45; there were practitioners in their 50s and 60s whose medical school years had been at the threshold of modern scientific medicine and who might have had little instruction in bacteriology or biochemistry. They would have resented those coming out of Harvard, Yale, Hopkins, or Michigan, and would not have understood much that they were talking about. They would have feared competition from the newcomers who knew so much and whose knowledge seemed so marvelous to their patients. It was a time when faith in scientific progress was running high, and the modern doctor in the eyes of many was the epitome of the scientific man. Peabody pointed to the "amazing progress of science in its relation to medicine during the last thirty years," but went on to give the "practitioner of the older generation" his due: there was much in his art to teach the new crowd.

Thier, I believe, referred to criticism coming from without, the questioning of biomedical science and technology that has stubbornly persisted, especially among those who came of age in the '60s, as well as among some social scientists and public health people whose concern is more with denominators than with numerators, with populations rather than individuals.

Medical schools have tried to resolve this problem by bringing in the humanities, and by urging undergraduates not to neglect history, literature, languages, and philosophy during their four years of college. All of this is good for education and adds to the quality of the physician's life, but there are no data showing that humanists are more humane than scientists or better practitioners of the art.

Peabody and Thier came to similar conclusions: the merging of science and art occurs in the clinic or at the bedside or not at all. "The treatment of a disease may be entirely impersonal; the care of a patient must be completely personal," wrote Peabody, and he might have added that the care of patients is no less important because there is "nothing the matter with them." Indeed it was these patients with their headaches and backaches, belly pains and insomnia, depression and anxieties that always baffled young physicians from academic teaching hospitals, whether in 1989 or 1927.

Dismiss them with a "There's really nothing the matter with you," or knock them low with diazepam, and they will soon dismiss the whole profession and seek help from some "alternative" practitioner. When science fails, they, and even we, may turn to magic. But the skillful physician has something more than science, never to use in its place, yet not magic either, and that is his understanding of what Osler called "this deliciously credulous old human nature in which we work." These things are taught and learned at the bedside and in the clinics, and for those with eyes to see them, in novels, plays, and poetry, but rarely in behavioral science courses. They are taught mostly by example and learned only by experience.

REFERENCES

1. Peabody FW: The care of the patient. *JAMA* 1927; 88:887–2.
2. Thier SO: The range of significant issues in medicine. In: *The Medical Profession: Enduring and New Challenges.* Medical Education Group, AMA; 1987:23–30.

Connecticut Medicine 1989; 53(2):119

Night Thoughts on End-of-the Century Medicine

TO see ourselves as others see us is rarely granted, but when a loved one becomes a patient and the sickness is grave there can be no escaping some reflections on medicine, even though we know that our vision at such times is refracted by anxiety and impatience. What we see and feel as both physician and spouse is not the stuff of which generalizations should be made. The experience of an unexpected, possibly mortal illness in one's life partner forces a physician to examine, perhaps at too close range, the forms and rituals of his own profession as well as the motives of those who try to control it. Time will soften my impressions but by then they will have lost something of their sharpness and clarity.

Physicians, at least most of the physicians I have known, are smart, thoughtful, caring people. Some have more empathy than others; some show a remarkably different *persona* at the bedside from that at cocktail parties or staff meetings. Their masks are both amusing and troubling; you don't want your physicians at such times to be thinking about how they are coming across, but rather to be attending single-mindedly to the problem at hand. This role playing is often evident and clumsy in physicians in training, but even old hands may put on a mask, making you wonder whether you have known your colleague as well as you thought. And then we reflect that we too have play-acted at such times; it's just that we felt confident that we were better at it!

Patient autonomy is in and paternalism is out; that is as it should be. But patients, struggling in the midst of a devastating event, certain to diminish their lives forever, find it painful with their limited knowledge to decide between two courses of treatment. Informed consent, informed, that is, by a few minutes of talk, must often be a vain ritual. It is her physician's judgment she now wants to hear, even though she may question it or disagree; her right to autonomy is far from her mind when life may be at stake.

Continuity of care is an ideal we instill in our medical students from their first few months in medical school; it is not, unfortunately, much regarded in teaching hospitals. With the endless parade of consultants, fellows, residents, and students, many of whom are seen but once, the bewildered patient abandons all efforts to decide who is in charge and finds her security in the familiar face of a friendly PGY-l [postgraduate year 1], who two days later rotates off service. Others come and go, unidentified, without name tags or identifying dress—strangers, without introductions, calling a patient they have never before seen by her first name, asking all the same tiresome questions again and again and again, then disappearing forever. Even a critically-ill patient knows there is something terribly inefficient in all this, and asks her physician-husband to explain. "Are we paying for this? Surely somebody is!"

In the midst of the incessant noise, incivility, and inefficiency of the modern hospital there are among the mostly disinterested crowd a few blessed souls, perhaps nurse aides, lab technicians, therapists, nurses, or even physicians, whose faces, voices, and hands display genuine empathy and equanimity, qualities that are not contrary, but rather often associated in company with extraordinary competence. These are the marks by which the patient recognizes her healers; all of the other amazements of modern medicine and the modern hospital are mostly lost on her, or may be seen as irrelevancies. Of one elegant and expensive procedure to which she declined to submit, she told the physician it was quite obviously of no use to her but only for "your entertainment and enlightenment!"

Most of this changed in the quietly efficient rehabilitation unit of a well-run nursing home. Here was a place to get well in; the increase in empathy and attention to the serious business of caring was everywhere unmistakable. Some of the hospital culture persisted, but civility and quiet had mostly replaced the cocktail-party racket of the 1990s hospital. It is a mercy that hospital lengths-of-stay have been reduced to less than a week; any benefits that might be gained there would be lost if the economics of a longer stay in such places improved some insurance company's bottom line!

Rereading Walter Pater's description of a temple of Aesculapius in *Marius the Epicurean* evokes visions of a modern hospital with all its wonderfully effective technology somehow incorporated into a place of healing where "Simply to be alive and there was a delight. . . . the air of the room about him seemed like pure gold, the very shadows rich with colour."

Connecticut Medicine 1995; 59(3):183

Medicine: Are We on the Threshhold of Another Golden Age?

FORTY-FIVE years ago when I was studying for the Boards in medicine, the received wisdom had been to read (and if possible memorize) the *Year Book of Medicine* and all the editorials in the *Annals of Internal Medicine*, in addition, of course, to knowing backward and forward your Cecil and Loeb *Textbook of Medicine*. Mine was the 1951 edition, already out of date. But that could be compensated for by reading the *Year Book*.

I recently thumbed through the 1951 *Year Book of Medicine* whose editors were a distinguished crowd indeed: Paul B. Beeson, J. Burns Amberson, William B. Castle, Tinsley R. Harrison, and George B. Eusterman. The important clinical news was the recognition of bacterial resistance to antibiotics. Beeson comments, " . . . an unsettling discussion. One wonders what place penicillin, aureomycin, *et al* will have 10 years from now." The role of ACTH and cortisone in infection seemed confusing. A group at the Mayo Clinic found what they thought was a beneficial clinical effect in treating pneumonia by using both ACTH and penicillin; the prompt defervescence and clinical improvement was not associated, however, with any decline in the number of organisms in the sputum. The authors decided not to recommend it.

Gamma globulin was being tried in polio, and "appears to be more practical to use than a vaccine." Beeson commented on "frequent statements in newspapers, some . . . by responsible persons, indicating that an effective vaccine is about to be perfected."

Do you remember Bornholm disease? Epidemic pleurodynia—there was an entire section on this, including a report of a laboratory outbreak in London that suggested Coxsackie virus 2 as the etiologic agent. That year we diagnosed this disease all over the place.

Still controversial was the pathophysiology of rheumatic fever, in fact, of all collagen diseases: the place of salicylates in treatment, the role of ACTH and cortisone, and the part that penicillin might play in prevention or treatment. Belief that foci of infection were either the cause of or played some part in ill-defined aches, pains, and fatigue, as well as in more serious conditions, such as iridocyclitis, rheumatoid arthritis, and glomerulonephritis, had been around since 1912. The faith was waning by 1950, but it was hard for many of us to let go.

Pulmonary tuberculosis filled 26 pages in the 1951 *Yearbook*, compared with 38 pages five years earlier, and six pages two decades later. Even though streptomycin and para-aminosalicylic acid in combination were beginning to look promising, bed rest, surgery, and collapse therapy remained the mainstays of treatment. Disappointment with streptomycin therapy in tuberculous meningitis led to a trial with combined therapy using tuberculin intrathecally. Dr. Beeson found this "an exciting idea," and recommended further trial "by capable clinicians." Robert Koch had promoted his tuberculin as a cure for tuberculosis 60 years earlier.

Hypertension appeared to result from renal ischemia and the release of renin; this was still the Goldblatt Era, although Hans Selye implicated the pituitary as mediating the stress response through the adrenals. Treatment for severe hypertension included the Smithwick operation of sympathectomy, especially if there was papilledema, or perhaps a trial of potassium thiocyanate or one of the veratrum alkaloids; otherwise weight reduction, low protein, and a "very low sodium diet." These were the years of the Kempner rice diet; drugs other than mild sedatives were rarely used. The recommended dietary regimens differed little from those recently rediscovered and reported in the *New England Journal of Medicine* (April 17, 1997).

Except for some types of congenital heart disease, which by 1950 could be accurately diagnosed by cardiac catheterization, surgery had little place in treatment. Without question, however, the increased understanding of cardiac physiology after the more widespread use of venous catheterization of the right atrium and ventricle was the most exciting news of the time.

Drugs for congestive failure were still pretty much limited to digitalis, mercuhydrin, sometimes ammonium chloride, and quinidine. Tinsley Harrison was the editor for the section on the Heart and Blood Vessels and the Kidneys; he concluded the abstracts:

> The evidence that hypercholesterolemia, however induced, favors the production of atheromatous changes in the coronary (and other) arteries seems indisputable. . . .
>
> The old problem of the artificial kidney was attacked anew and may be approaching a solution. . . .
>
> To the philosopher (or in the present instance, the pseudophilosopher) certain conclusions seem to emerge from this brief survey of the rapid progress made in the cardiovascular field during the past decade. The first is that few problems in medicine are inherently insoluble. If the problem of bacterial endocarditis can be largely solved, if blue babies can live to

> be pink adults, if persons with congestive heart failure can be kept alive for many years and often for decades, if an optimistic viewpoint toward . . . atherosclerosis has emerged, it would be folly to believe that disorders which now seem totally hopeless will remain so (p. 477).

The etiology of peptic ulcer was admittedly unknown, although few doubted the sequence of stress, vasoconstriction in the gastric antrum and the duodenum, hypo- or anoxemia of the tissues, vagus stimulation, increased gastric secretions including acid and pepsin, and finally necrosis and ulceration. Increasing dissatisfaction with the Sippy regimen of whole milk or cream and absorbable antacids resulted in trials with protein hydrolysates and all manner of antacid salts of magnesium, aluminum, and calcium. One gastric hemorrhage or perforation meant a subtotal gastrectomy and most likely a vagotomy.

No question, those were simpler days. You could count the useful drugs on the fingers of your two hands. RNA and DNA were mostly unheard of. That DNA carried some sort of genetic information had been known as early as 1944; however, not until 1953 did Francis Crick and James D. Watson show that the DNA molecule was a double helix. Cellular and molecular biology were barely on the horizon for most of us, and we begged for crash courses from our friendly biochemist colleagues. How hormones worked, why some bacteria and viruses caused disease, what the mechanism of inflammation and immunity was—all this was beyond us. Cells had membranes, cytoplasm, a nucleus, and some funny thing called a Golgi apparatus. What else was there to know?

We all sensed, however, that we were at the beginning of amazing times in science, in space, and in medicine, and indeed during the spring clinical meetings in Atlantic City we often agreed over cocktails that we were lucky to be living in the Golden Age of medicine.

In another half century, in 2047, medical residents studying today for their boards will be pushing four-score years. With successful aging, many may still be in practice. Society will have moved out of its doldrums by then; medical care will be as universal as air and will have broken free from its destructive liaison with the insurance industry; funding for research will once again be in ascendancy.

Science for 4 April 1997, with its cover illustrating the Prometheus myth, featured in its "Frontiers in Medicine" the regeneration of tissues, organs, and even eyes and limbs, reminding its readers of that unhappy Titan who, after stealing fire from Olympus to give to mankind, was punished by Zeus by being chained to a pillar in the Caucuses where a vulture tore at his liver all day, year in and year out; and there was no end to the pain because every night his liver grew whole again.

Surely to know how to regenerate organs would be almost the end of all our seeking, to be able not merely to transplant but to grow new organs in patients who had lost a critical part of one of theirs to trauma or disease. The possibilities, to use a figure of the 17th-century physician Thomas Browne, stretch the *Pia Mater* almost to its breaking! How many of us have wondered why worms and cockroaches and amphibians should have denied to us, their mammalian descendents, this special blessing.

They didn't withhold the secret entirely. Removing two thirds of the liver in rats is followed by regeneration, if intact lobes are left behind, and is complete in five to seven days. Even in dogs and human beings regeneration is proportional to the amount of liver mass removed. This is not new, but unraveling the mechanisms is. Stem cells in the brain have been identified that may, when the mechanism is better understood, provide the means for reconstructing the diseased or injured brain or cord.

Some amphibians can regenerate organs and complex structures, new limbs, parts of the heart, retinas and lenses; that is beyond the capacity of the rest of us vertebrates. But the relatively new sciences of cellular and molecular biology have tackled problems as tough as this before.

Exciting indeed, but we still have work to do to make the best use of what we already know. The American College of Physician's 15-year-old Clinical Efficacy Assessment Project (CEAP) has recommitted itself to evidence-based medicine, working in cooperation with the American Heart Association and the American Academy of Pediatrics. Nothing new here: Pierre Louis in 1835, by studying the course of the disease in many cases of pneumonia, erysipelas, and tonsillitis, was able to show that the universal treatment of the time, blood-letting, simply made no difference in outcomes. Before we go too far in writing standards for care in our overgrown late 20th-century medicine, we too need better evidence that what we do makes a difference. Pierre Louis' work led to something like therapeutic nihilism. This is not tenable today, of course, but a little touch of it might be salutary for both patients and those who pay the bills.

Connecticut Medicine 1997; 61(5):305–6

Section 3—Medical Ethics and Principles

The last temptation is the greatest treason: to do the right deed for the wrong reason.

T.S. Eliot (1888–1965)

Ethics, too, are nothing but reverence for life.

Albert Schweitzer (1875–1965)

Virtues, Not Values: Medical Ethics, Not Business *Ethos*

FOR the past several months virtues have had an unexpected media boost. The pope asserted, in effect, that democracy could not work in the absence of virtue. Programs are being marketed to schools, audio tapes to be broadcast over classroom loudspeakers, proclaiming honesty, self-respect, hard work, and decent living. Hundreds of thousands of black males marched in an action of atonement and resolved to lead new and virtuous lives. There is a growing sense that the flimsy secular morality of the late 20th century, while helpful for a peaceable community, will never assure it. The much maligned Victorians proclaimed a more comprehensive moral requirement; in Thackeray's words, one should aspire

> . . . to have lofty aims, to lead a pure life, to keep your honour virgin; to have the esteem of your fellow citizens, and the love of your fireside; to bear good fortune meekly; to suffer evil with constancy; and through evil or good to maintain truth always.

Recent nonbiased historical studies have shown that those Victorians and Edwardians really meant all this! There is little question that the 18th- and early 19th-century American Republic took for granted the morals and manners of its citizenry, and depended on a shared ethical code to make their democracy work. The Enlightenment was followed by the Great Awakening!

Before biomedical ethics arrived on the scene about 30 years ago, our profession had assumed that doctors were, by and large, committed to something like the Victorian virtues; the easy acquiescence of many of our German and other European colleagues during the Nazi years raised grave doubts about these assumptions of integrity. After the war, undreamed of new procedures and technologies presented ethical problems that seemed to overwhelm the simpler virtue ethics of our Victorian grandfathers.

The new bioethics, with its mantra of autonomy, nonmalfeasance, beneficence and justice, nevertheless, dealt as medical ethics always had, with the rights and responsibilities of that ancient duality, the doctor and patient or the nurse and patient. Little attention was paid to the laws of the guild in the new ethics, and the barrier that separated medicine from out-and-out commercialism slowly crumbled. Doctors and hospitals began to advertise their product lines and to talk of marketing strategy, market share, and delivering health care rather than providing medical care; the whole enterprise came to refer to itself as the health-care industry and paid its managers corporate salaries. The burden of nonprofit status was lightened by restructuring. Competition was the rule of the marketplace, and cooperation was out the window.

The *ethos* of corporations is hardly the same as the ethics of medicine. Neither is the *ethos* of big government: profit drives the corporation and politics is the energy of government. But the care of the sick, the disturbed, and the vulnerable should require that the ethics of medicine bind the institutions who profit by their outstanding skill in managing just as they bind the only ones who provide that care.

Institutional review boards, in other words, should begin reviewing their institutions. HMOs, group practices, hospitals, nursing homes, surgicenters, academic medical centers, and insurance companies who manage care and handle the money all for profit, now, more than ever before, need an immersion in classical medical and nursing ethics. Virtues, not values, are enjoying a rebirth; ethics committees should latch on to this new enthusiasm for doing the right things for the right reasons.

They might start with the list in the Hippocratic Oath: defend the solidarity of the guild, use simple treatment measures first according to our ability and judgment, keep our patients from harm *and injustice*, give no deadly drugs *even if asked*, live a life and practice an art *in purity and holiness*, never attempt what we do not know how to do, remember that all our work is *only* for the *benefit* of the sick, and finally keep all in strictest confidence (I have left out the line on abortion because that stirs controversy wherever moral strangers meet).

The Oath is but the beginning. Autonomy, or permission, beneficence, nonmaleficence or nonmalevolence, and justice—all add to and overlap the oath. But to these must be added charity; to paraphrase St. Paul: if I "have not charity, I am nothing." Corporate medicine may interpret this as charitable giving, funding professorships and beds and sponsoring AIDS research, but all that "profiteth nothing." Virtues, practiced with *caritas*, must be built into, become a part of, those corporations who have risked their capital to manage the practice of medicine; otherwise they should turn to managing something else, like highway repairs or parks and grounds. Surely, virtues rather than values are the coming thing!

Connecticut Medicine 1995; 59(11):689

A Matter of Principle

But our principles demanded it, and convinced of their virtue,
I strove always to be consistent to them.

Stanhope Forbes (1857–1947)

IN her brief essay on *The Health of the Bride*, the painting reproduced on the cover of *JAMA* for June 7, 1985, Kathryn Simmons quoted the artist, Stanhope Forbes, who had written, in 1898, that his artistic creed was "to paint our pictures directly from Nature and not merely to rely upon sketches and studies which we could afterwards amplify in the comfort of a studio." He observed that this was not always easy to do, Nature being what she was.

Some of our first-year medical students in their seminar on the quality of medical care have been wrestling with this matter of principles. In trying to make sense out of this year's fashion—HMOs, DRGs, PPOs, vertical and horizontal reorganization, and on and on—they quickly discover the flaw, the absence of principle, as they come to ask about what is behind this or that scheme, and how it will affect the behavior of physicians, hospital administrators, insurance companies, and patients.

"I'm going to do what I think is right no matter what the bureaucrats or administrators say!"

"Then what if you lose your privileges, or they tell you you can't work for their group or hospital anymore, or Medicare won't pay you?" asks another student.

"So be it. I want to be able to sleep nights."

There are signs of agreement all around, but they know that it will be years before they face the difficult professional choices. Today, the principles are still holding, the idealism that lighted and guided their way into medical school is just now facing the barest suggestion of a challenge.

Principles, like virtue, have fallen from fashion and from intellectual grace; too often when someone begins talking up the "principle of the thing," he is about to get himself into or out of some unprincipled act. But trying to make decisions without principles is like trying to do geometry without axioms.

A cartoon in one of the medical newspapers last spring showed a wrecker's ball being swung against the house of medicine; the implication was that the whole enterprise was about to come down; everyone was scrambling to have a say in whatever was to follow. The scrambling certainly is evident, but my hunch is that it is going nowhere. There is a standoff between the doctors on the one hand and all of the government, business, and investor interests on the other who stand to gain financially from the outcome. The doctors are looking for their principles; they remember that they had them when they came into medicine; they recall, with Osler, that "the profession of medicine is distinguished from all others by its singular beneficence."

In an earlier and simpler time we quoted the greats and were satisfied that we had made our point. No one needed to explain Francis Peabody. We appealed to universal principles, but now in an age of moral relativism, one principle is as good or bad as another, and consequently none is good for much of anything. When the vision of the Grail turns out to be an illusion, what's wrong with replacing it with a bottom line? One of my colleagues said recently that "it looks as though medicine is about to join the real world."

If so, we agreed that whatever esteem medicine had earned came from the "unreal" world we were about to leave, where some principles were better than others, and even the unprincipled knew the difference; where those who were troubled, in pain, sick, and helpless could expect to be cared for by men and women whose single-minded aim was "to cure sometimes, to relieve often, to comfort always."

The principle that making money should never come ahead of that obligation is so ancient as to need no defense, yet it is that principle that is under fire. No one pretends that all physicians have always been faithful, but most have acknowledged the principle, and their patients have counted on it.

"No one should approach the temple of science with the soul of a money changer," wrote Sir Thomas Browne in the 17th century. [The Swiss-born physician and alchemist] Paracelsus in the century before condemned the practitioner who worked "not out of love for the patient, which should be the physician's first virtue, but for the sake of money. Where money is the goal, envy and hatred, pride and conceit, are sure to appear. . . ."

Connecticut Medicine 1985; 49(11):763

The Nothnagel Principle

Only a good man can be a great physician.

Hermann Nothnagel (1841–1905)

WHEN Dr. Alexander Menzer announced his retirement from pediatric practice in West Hartford recently, he recalled Hermann Nothnagel's brief axiom from his Vienna medical school days. Dr. Menzer is 80 years old but that statement of principle relating medicine and virtue had stuck. In late August, at the Jay Healey Convocation for new medical and dental students at the University of Connecticut, Dr. Sherwin Nuland recalled this ancient principle in his address to the members of the classes of 1999: "Only a good man can be a great physician." Perhaps they already knew it, but we live at a time when the notion exists that our off-duty lives are nobody's business but our own as long as we do our jobs reasonably well.

Perhaps this axiom should be called the Nothnagel Principle. But its origins go back to a time much earlier than 1882 and the glory days of the Vienna Medical School: it was already ancient in our profession in the days of Galen. Remember the line in the Hippocratic Oath: "In purity and in holiness will I guard my life and my art."

At this point a late 20th-century ethicist is sure to ask you for a definition of "good." He will ask you to tell him what Professor Nothnagel meant by "a great physician"! Fair enough. Either question could start a Socratic dialogue, the difference being that Socrates and his crowd of young Athenians were attempting to get at the Truth. Today's philosopher will tell you that there are many truths, just as "ethics" is plural, with few unquestionably right answers. He is apt to tell you this using a language that only another ethicist can claim to understand, or else leave you wondering if the answer really matters.

Nothnagel's view of the world, according to the medical historian Erna Lesky, was "inspired by his humanism and nurtured by German classicism."[1] In other words, his ethical system derived from Kant and Hegel, Plato and Aristotle, all against a background of Augustine and Luther, for each of whom Truth was an absolute discoverable by reason (at times assisted by grace). But my guess is that he learned to discern right from wrong and to do the right thing as a child at home in Alt-Lietzegöricke in Brandenburg. Men and women, good or bad, in the 19th- and early 20th-century were quite sure of the content of their common ethics, and believed they could recognize the good, the true, and the beautiful even without rehearsing Kant or Rousseau.

Present doubts about our willingness to agree on a common morality are compelling evidence that we are leaving one age behind and stumbling half blinded into the next, which today we may call either "postmodern" or the "New Age," depending on a point of view that will change tomorrow. Is it any wonder that we make a virtue out of necessity, extolling multiculturalism, pluralism, and ethical relativism as manifestations of enlightenment? If you don't know "where you want to get to," said the Cat. . . . "then it doesn't matter which way you go" [Lewis Carroll, *Alice's Adventure in Wonderland*].

But we have been thinking only of philosophers and ethicists, politicians, journalists, academicians, and other opinion makers—surely no more than five percent of the population. Those students who heard Dr. Nothnagel speak of the connection between being a good person and a great doctor, as well as those who heard Dr. Nuland more than a century later remind them of the great traditions of our profession and the Nothnagel Principle, understood what had been said. Dr. Menzer knew what he meant by "a good person" when he quoted the Viennese professor. Our patients, too, few of whom spend time thinking about autonomy and beneficence, know good and evil when they see it.

The goodness they know is more than moral rules and ethical reasoning, as important to our understanding as these may be. Goodness has to do with how lives are lived, and for whom and to what purpose. Robert Coles wrote somewhere that each of us is a whole, undivided person, that we cannot be amoral or unloving in one part of our lives and great physicians in another. Even if our students learn to be technically elegant, intellectually unchallengeable, and politically and socially correct, if they are not good citizens, good fathers and mothers, good husbands and wives, and good friends and lovers, their medical lives will be dry as dust, and their patients will have been cheated, even perhaps at risk.

REFERENCE

1. Lesky E: *The Vienna Medical School of the 19th Century*. Baltimore: The Johns Hopkins University Press; 1976:279–90.

Connecticut Medicine 1995; 59(9):565

Rule 6, Never Take Yourself Seriously

IF I mention William Carlos Williams to medical students, some recall him as a modern American poet, one or two know that he was a physician, and most have never heard of him. These students went to high school in the late 1980s and early 1990s. So much for education in the postmodern, multiculturalist era. Those who may know a little of his work often remember *The Red Wheelbarrow*:[1]

so much depends
upon

a red wheel
barrow

glazed with rain
water

beside the white
chickens

Williams (1883–1963) is of the generation of medical students' great-grandfathers, a time that must seem to 23-year-olds inconceivably ancient and mostly irrelevant. Yet he was one of the most highly esteemed neomodernist poets; another physician neomodernist poet was Gertrude Stein (1874–1946); one difference between them, among many, was that he was a real doctor, really practiced medicine!

> It's the humdrum, day in, day out, everyday work that is the real satisfaction of the practice of medicine; the million and a half patients a man has seen on his daily visits over a 40-year period of weekdays and Sundays that make up his life. I have never had a money practice; it would have been impossible for me.[2]

For him literature and medicine stood on the same footing, and were taken equally seriously. "That is why as a writer I have never felt that medicine interfered with me," he wrote, "but rather that it was my food and drink."

In many medical schools the humanities have in one way or another been reintroduced to students as a kind of balance in their lives, complementing the "everyday work" of medicine and showing that their universe can be seen through other lenses than molecular biology and how to survive in a managed-care world. *The Red Wheelbarrow* creates, I suspect, almost the same vivid image in everyone's mind, red, white, and rain, not at all hard to see and describe. Some will immediately observe that the poem doesn't make a sentence, maybe doesn't make sense, that there should be a "that" after "chickens," a conclusion to "so much depends upon. . . ." But then it is easy to drop that conversation, not much to say, and move on.

From Williams's own comments about it we know that he meant something profoundly important by these 16 words: that so much, everything in fact, depends on small everyday, commonplace things, like chickens and rain and wheelbarrows. In that sense, his autobiographical sentences about the everyday, humdrum work of medicine making up a life and the red wheelbarrow and the rain and the chickens mean the same thing.

Winston Churchill, it was rumored, had a set of rules that he expected his associates, as well as himself, to live by. One of them, Rule 6, he said, was never take yourself seriously. When asked by someone newly appointed to his staff what the other rules were, he looked up and answered, "There aren't any."

My impression is that the managed-care outfits, especially those who are in it for the money, take themselves terribly seriously. And why shouldn't they? Dollars are pretty serious, especially to CEOs and stockholders, and, after all, someone has to manage the practice of medicine (the delivery of health care, sorry). And manage the doctors and the nurses and the technicians and all the others who are just doing their ordinary, everyday work. The trouble is it's in the nature of managers to manage other people's work. To keep you healthy. Health maintenance they call it. What nonsense.

The "humdrum, day in, day out, everyday work" of medicine is all that should matter, is all anyway that matters to patients. Dr. Williams might say, "so much depends upon" listening to a troubled patient, reading an EKG, repairing a hernia, prescribing penicillin, easing a pain, or just being there when the call comes, and leave it at that. But then, he would be the last person ever to take himself seriously, to preach a sermon, but if he did, he'd make it short and call it a homily.

REFERENCES

1. *The Selected Poems of William Carlos Williams*. New York: New Directions Publishing Company; 1968:30.
2 Quoted in Cousins N, ed. *The Physician in Literature*. Philadelphia: W.B. Saunders Company; 1982:310.

Connecticut Medicine 1996; 60(5):309

Surrendering Clinical Judgment

IN a lecture to our students and faculty, a visiting professor of bioethics warned that physicians were turning their important decisions over to lawyers and accountants, giving up the ground that was uniquely theirs, setting aside their special right to make clinical judgments.

Talk of the ethics of terminating life support turns quickly to a discussion of the legal issues: let's call the attorney. And what about costs? Too much life support will surely bankrupt the family, increase the insurance rates, and ruin the hospital. No doubt that clinical judgment must include all these considerations: it concerns the life and well-being of a person, it includes a whole universe: "There is all of Africa and her prodigies in us," wrote Browne, and later, "Whilst I study to find how I am a microcosm, or little world, I find myself something more than the great."[1]

According to Hippocrates, clinical judgment is difficult. It is more than drawing decision trees or making probability guesses on a list of diagnoses and therapeutic outcomes. It is not the scientific method transposed from the laboratory to the bedside, nor is it intuition, nor remarkably keen special senses. Nor is it essentially a fine moral sensitivity coupled with whatever one learns when he is taught problem solving instead of facts. It does depend in part upon the knowledge which physicians acquire in their education and experience and which is shared by no one else. For that reason, others cannot possess it entirely; lawyers, accountants, philosophers, and patients have special knowledge which physicians may not have, but they do not have what is needed for making clinical judgments.

Mostly they do not pretend to it either. But with business coalitions telling us how hospitals should be run, with telephone hot-lines to our masters in Washington, with lawyers, accountants, regulators, and a whole host of guardians all over the place, there may be no occasion for doctors to make clinical judgments; instead they become merely skillful technicians responding to faceless controllers all acting in the public interest.

The troubling thing is that all this is happening gradually enough so that most of us hardly notice; those who speak out in warning are quickly silenced as eccentrics or troublemakers. Each age, I suspect, loses some value or ideal without anyone, except maybe the poets and some of the historians, ever taking note. The past often assumes a rosy glow, but that mostly has to do with our talent for forgetting the bad things. The ancients told of golden ages, always in the past; sometimes, as after the age of Pericles, they were right, but more often these times were only reflections out of the memories of old men.

The values and *mores* of the past slip easily from memory; it is as though we lose our receptors for certain words or concepts, cannot even recall what meanings they used to carry. We rarely speak of medicine as a *calling* in these times, and the word *vocation* has nothing like the meaning it carried only a 100 years ago. Because there are no other words for that meaning to attach itself to, the notion of being *called* to a service becomes meaningless. When physicians think of themselves as deliverers of health care, and patients are clients, then clinical judgment and ultimate concern for the patient's welfare may no longer be in anybody's mind.

There are signs that this may be turning around. Medical ethics now means something more serious than it did 30 years ago. Medical students are uncomfortable when they see us preoccupied with money; our faculty members are reaffirming their commitment to students, to their education, and to honest science. Even though values may slip away imperceptibly, some kind of early warning device gets turned on, usually in the young who, as they grow up, will almost certainly rediscover their grandfathers if we will only let them.

REFERENCE

1. Browne, Sir Thomas: *Religio Medici,* Part I, Sect XV; Part II, Sect XI; 1643.

Connecticut Medicine 1984; 48(1):57

Weather Patterns

IN an informal discussion among clinicians and basic scientists, someone asked if there were a new breed of internist. I recalled an earlier conversation in which a professor at another medical school said that the generation of academic physicians who had come of age during the two decades following World War II had been a different breed (he referred to that period as a "blip"), and that we are now returning to normal. An eminent biomedical scientist said that medicine had taken a wrong turn during those decades, and that we should have to pay for that mistake.

I would not quote anyone on this issue, not even myself, because observations like these are intended to provoke good conversation and may not be entirely serious, but they do suggest that change is in the air.

We have known that for some time. We sense changing political and social climate long before the weather front is upon us. No one would deny that there is a conservative mood in the western world; it may represent only a short rest in the midst of a period of exhaustingly rapid change, or it may be the beginning of a long quiet after a century of war, revolution, and technological excesses. We should need a special kind of satellite to see the social climate as clearly as we now can watch the terrestrial weather.

These times are of concern to the medical educator. The cries demanding change are in swaying balance with the voices insisting that we hold fast at any cost. Decision is perilous, there are never enough data, and in a time of change it seems as though all our values get caught up in the storm.

I believe it only seems that way, and unless we are thoroughgoing relativists, we must believe that some values, the important ones, remain in place even at the end of a civilization. And as for facts, once a thing has been proved, it stays proved. Most change, especially social change, may be quite superficial, except for those long historical sweeps that are too slow to perceive in a single lifetime.

"I buy an American journal, anything. *Harper's* magazine, the first article I happen to notice: "The Crisis of Medical Service." At once I find myself in the midst of the problem. Medicine has become too expensive, has become a commodity that can no longer be afforded. A new system of medical service must be found." Henry Sigerist wrote that in his diary almost 50 years ago.[1] Eight years later he wrote, "Today the President read a message to

Congress recommending the National Health Program which includes compulsory health insurance."[1(144)]

During the decades following World War II, medicine and society invested heavily in biomedical research. In the late 60s prominent physicians were announcing their discovery that medicine was a social science (which Virchow had observed over a 100 years earlier). Later, medicine was recognized as one of the humanities, and now its status as a clinical science (or art) has been rediscovered.

That recurring cycle is to be expected. Medicine is too vast and too deep to be seen whole and all at one time. Whichever of its aspects is ascendant will depend upon what we are prepared to see in the light of current social or political fashions. Try as we will, we cannot pull away from those forces and deny that we are being vouchsafed a new revelation.

Each new insight seems far better, more honest and true, than yesterday's insight, and clearly an improvement over what had been believed a decade ago. This is some kind of a law and the basis for fashion. Consequently when our rhetoricians discover clinical medicine, they appear to be denouncing science and technology; and when they rediscover science, for effect they must scoff, slightly, at clinical judgment. The clinician Sydenham and the scientist Harvey shared the same century but barely acknowledged one another.

The subject of all of our endeavors remains the same, however, and because that subject is a living organism, a member of the human family, and a person, medicine remains both an art and a science, beginning and ending in philosophy. The breed of physicians remains essentially the same, but varieties are brought forth by the changing social weather.

REFERENCE

1. Sigerist HE: *Autobiographical Writings*. Montreal: McGill University Press; 1966:70–2 (September 17, 1931).

Connecticut Medicine 1979; 43(6):396

The Passing of Sunday Peace

> Six days shalt thou labor and do all thy work: But the seventh is the Sabbath of the LORD thy God: *in it* thou shalt not do any work.
>
> *Exodus xx: 9, 10.*

> It being contrary to the law and disagreeable to the People of this State (Connecticut) to travel on the Sabbath day—and my horses, after passing through such intolerable roads, wanting rest, I stayed at Perkins' tavern.
>
> *The Diary of George Washington, 8 November 1789*

IN these latter days of the 20th century, an obligatory day of rest, like so many other ancient and beneficent customs, has faded from common memory. Growing up in Detroit, in a family that prided itself on its modern ideas, even going so far as to discuss Darwin at Sunday dinner to shock my fundamentalist aunt, I was never allowed to forget that Sunday was the Sabbath. No movies, no card playing, and no unnecessary work. We knew some Seventh Day Adventists who cut their grass on Sunday, and I might walk to a nearby delicatessen for cold cuts and rye bread for Sunday supper. But on that day I never had to mow the lawn or dig dandelions or put up the storm windows. Even homework was discouraged: "Surely you could have done that yesterday or Friday!" Assigned reading was not really work.

Sunday afternoon was for driving into the country or to Belle Isle or taking the ferry to Bob-Lo Island. No stores were open, except Sanders' Ice Cream where you could get a sundae, a dish they had invented for the after church crowd on Sunday! If the day was rainy, we listened to the radio, light classical music usually, and my father and I played chess, but never a card game. In the evening we all sat in the study and listened to the Ford Sunday Evening Hour, Jack Benny, and Fred Allen. Or my mother played the piano and we sang from some book called "Favorite Tunes." Sunday felt different from the other six days, entirely separate, and the city too had a peaceable look.

The Jews and later the Christians introduced the Mediterranean world to the rule of one day of rest out of seven, for everyone, even slaves. For the Jews it was *shabbat,* for the Christians, the Lord's day. After the conversion of the Roman Empire, Constantine in 321 A.D. declared Sunday a day of rest, a decree later repeated in the Code of Justinian. For the Jews the origin of *shabbat* observance is lost in antiquity, but was formalized after the Exile. Few institutions have relieved the lot of humankind more than this one, condemned, or blessed, as we are to labor for our daily bread. In an agrarian society it was a blessing to feel good about not working on this one day in seven. Sabbath signified that there was more to life than work.

Something of the Sabbath peace prevailed even in hospitals. As a house officer I recall the relief that followed the Saturday discharges, the sense of time stretching out until Sunday evening when admissions would begin to pile in. Sunday mornings were quiet, rounds later and leisurely, time to catch up on charts, time to spend with patients, time to read the *New England Journal of Medicine,* bring your wife in for Sunday dinner in the residents' dining room, or just take a nap. Hospital weekends still are slower, but, I suspect, not for long. Our new masters, the HMOs and insurance giants, will see to that. Pausing, even a little, for a Sabbath rest cuts into profits.

The retail world has shown how profitable it is to keep going seven days a week, sometimes 24 hours a day. Both parents, or the only parent, may be working on the one day the children are at home, or if they are not working, they are out shopping or pursuing some solitary recreation. Seeing the full parking lots in the mall on Sundays, the crowds wandering to and fro seduced into buying and spending in these unlovely places, evokes a longing for that old, occasionally tedious, day of rest, a day with family, recurring every seven days and sustained by convention, or religion, and sometimes even by law.

The Blue Laws have had a bad press, and politically their return is unlikely, probably unconstitutional. Perhaps they could be reintroduced as a public health measure! Millennia ago the Sabbath had been made for man, but man and the Sabbath have been remade in our enlightened times to serve mammon. The decline of Sabbath observance is further evidence that progress is a myth, and that all we experience is change, as often for the worse as for the better, maybe more often!

Connecticut Medicine 1995; 59(8):502

Albert Schweitzer's Simple Philosophy

> For my philosophy is simple. It has only one subject, that we should become simpler and better human beings, that we should become more humane humans than we are.
>
> *Albert Schweitzer*[1]

MY view of Albert Schweitzer when I first read about him in the mid 1940s was that he must be the greatest man in the world. During medical school days I had a few recordings of him playing Bach on the organ—one, "Come sweet death" *(Komm' lieber Tod)* I used to play before examinations. After the war was over articles about him appeared in *Life,* the *New York Times* Book Review section, and several medical journals, and I wondered at this giant who was a physician, missionary, philosopher, theologian, authority on Goethe, a world authority on organ building, and a distinguished organist himself. I even found my chief resident in his office late one night reading *The Quest of the Historical Jesus*, and he told me more about this remarkable man who was, and still is, one of his heroes.

A few physician friends even spent time with Schweitzer, helping out with the care of patients at his hospital in Lambaréné in French Equatorial Africa. I always regretted that the closest I had managed to come to that experience was to read *On the Edge of the Primeval Forest*, which he had written in 1921.[2] Dr. Schweitzer died peacefully after a busy day's work at the age of 90 in 1965, though the hospital is still there, supported by an international foundation, and continuing the work that he began in 1913.

"Reverence for Life," the basis for his ethical thought, remains very much alive. This phrase, *Ehrfurcht vor dem Leben*, came to Schweitzer in 1915 during one of his many errands of mercy up the Ogowe River, "unforeseen and unsought. . . . Now I had found my way to the idea in which world- and life-affirmation and ethics are contained side by side!"

Ethical rules in medicine, or in living a life, derive from principles that we have more of less accepted, that in turn rest upon something "inchoate," as one writer described those notions of right and wrong buried somewhere deep in our psyches. Lewis Thomas suggested that we may have been determined by natural selection to cooperate and be altruistic, sharing these characteristics with other living creatures. Schweitzer wrote that he had been "struggling to find the elementary and universal conception of the ethical which I had not discovered in any philosophy. . . . Ethics is nothing else than reverence for life."

For him this was no inchoate notion but, rather arose from a deeply religious view of the world: "To have reverence in the face of life is to be in the grip of the eternal, unoriginated, forward-pushing will, which is the foundation of all being." Much of this he wrote before 1923; yet as late as 1964, in his 9th decade, he continued to hold fast to this "universal conception," writing that "The idea of Reverence for Life contains everything that expresses love, submission, compassion, the sharing of joy, and common striving for the good of all."

Medical students in Europe and America have begun to rediscover the depths to be found in the life and writings of this great physician, even though most can never follow in his steps.[1–3] His decision, made simply "one morning in the autumn of 1904" was in response to a request of the Paris Missionary Society that concluded, "'Men and women who can reply simply to the Master's call, "Lord, I am coming," those are the people whom the Church needs.' The article finished, I quietly began my work. My search was over."

Schweitzer then went on to earn his medical degree, still continuing his pastoral work and completing some of his most important theological writing. It was after this, during the long 60 years of work in Lambaréné, that he developed his ethical philosophy of Reverence for Life that is so much needed by the world today, and which is once more appealing to medical students and physicians.

REFERENCES

1. Robles HE, ed: Foreword by Rhena Schweitzer Miller. *Reverence for Life: The Words of Albert Schweitzer.* San Francisco: Harper Collins; 1993.
2. Schweitzer A: *On the Edge of the Primeval Forest & More from the Primeval Forest: Experiences and Observations of a Doctor in Equatorial Africa.* New York: The MacMillan Company; 1948.
3. Joy CR, ed: *Albert Schweitzer: An Anthology.* Boston, Massachusetts: The Beacon Press; 1947.

Connecticut Medicine 1994; 58(2):105–6

Doing Right or Being Right?

> . . . there really are bad guys and good guys. The good guys must learn to be vocal, active, and assertive. The bad guys already are. Neutralists must be feared because they can be used.
>
> *Solomon Papper*[1]

SOLOMON Papper was the first chairman of medicine at the then new University of New Mexico School of Medicine, now almost 40 years ago. I had been involved in the early planning for the new school and played a small part in his recruitment; even before his arrival we had become good friends. Later we became close friends and colleagues, often lunching at some place remote from either of our institutions, especially when the conversation might be conspiratorial! He was the first faculty member on board after the appointment of the founding dean, Reginald H. Fitz.

Sol chaired and I served on the first human research review committee, a new thing under the sun in those days, which served both the medical school and the Lovelace Clinic and Foundation, and together we worked out the guidelines for making judgments in what, for me at least, was new territory. Sol's knowledge of philosophic ethics was much deeper than mine. We learned quickly the dogmatic principles of the burgeoning field of medical ethics, today summarized in the mantra: autonomy, beneficence, nonmaleficence, and justice. But Sol kept returning to what he called etiquette, the "little ethics," the day-to-day habits of the good physician and good person.

I soon understood what he meant by his "little ethics," and the students and house staff slowly learned by their chief's example. Occasionally we made rounds with students and house staff together, sometimes at our place, more often at the Bernalillo County Indian Hospital or the VA which were the university's teaching hospitals. After we had entered a patient's room, Sol made the introductions, always including house officers and students, commented about her flowers or the weather or the view from the window of the Sandia Mountains, washed his hands, fluffed up her pillow, straightened the blankets, and almost always, I noticed, loosened the tight sheet at the foot of the bed. The medical history, Sol reminded us, was to find out "What is troubling you?" and "What kind of person are you?"—questions that were woven unobtrusively into an otherwise simple, friendly conversation. A brief but careful examination followed, plans for the day reviewed, and the patient was encouraged to ask any questions she might have. There was never a sense of urgency, no hint of "I'm a very busy guy, and I'm in a hurry." He often sat down at the bedside, maybe held the patient's hand, or offered her a glass of water. After rounds, we went back to his office, closed the door, and proceeded to review all the charts. No discussions of diagnosis, prognosis, or plans ever took place in the patients' rooms or in the hall where others might overhear.

The professor and chairman spent half his day in the clinic, the rest as an academician:

> I spend half my day or more on rounds, at conferences, talking medicine, reading, or writing. The effort to do so is great, but the hazard of being less of an internist . . . is greater.
>
> If we practice quality medicine on our inpatient services and in our ambulatory facilities, the clinical portion of our teaching programs for house staff and students will be largely accomplished. We can talk to house staff and students all we want about meticulous care, but unless we practice it and teach by example, our words are largely wasted. . . .
>
> If one believes that by far the best way to teach is by example, then the best way to teach humane scholarship is for the faculty to be humane and scholarly in their personal and professional behavior.[1]

Sol Papper was often humorously cynical about the arrogant nonsense that too often characterizes academic medicine, especially in its use of language that "has an increasing propensity to be indirect and obscure rather than to clarify," and "uses a glossary of terms in some variable ways, so that one must know the ground rules . . . to interpret what is said." Here are a few of his definitions of terms that are heard in almost all faculty meetings:

opportunity—A long shot.

challenge—A long shot without money or space.

resources—An incantational near substitute for money.

potential—Age 45, excellent training, and meager accomplishments.

team, team player—In the positive sense, this is someone who agrees with the dean or chairman. I have visions of somebody having a team sweater, a proper team haircut. In the negative sense (not a team player), he can be viewed as a conspirator.

influential—Big mouth.

multidisciplinary—Without leadership.

integrated—Fully organized but without content.

relevant—Quality not required.

multifaceted—Chaos.

participatory democracy—There are two types: (1) no voice for anyone; (2) voice for all: nothing done.
interdepartmental—Make certain medicine and surgery are not in leadership roles.
curriculum designs
lockstep—The old curriculum, whatever its form.
longitudinal—One step does not lead forward to another.
horizontal—See integrated.
spiral—Everything is screwed up.
low profile—Hiding from the combat zone.
paranoid—One who *usually* disagrees with the dean or chairman.
immature—One who *often* disagrees with the dean or chairman.
compromise—Least and lowest common denominator.
progress—Curriculum change.
essentially—Plus or minus 100 percent.
focus—Ignore everything except my point.
mission—Improve parking.
solution—Refer to a committee.

In his discussion of the arcane language of faculty meetings, he quoted Harry Truman: "If you can't convince them, confuse them."

Two principles guided Sol Papper's all too short life in medicine, and his colleagues and students heard them again and again: "Doing right as distinguished from being right in patient care is a practical issue and not one of philosophical abstraction. . . . Doing right has greater value because patient management and not diagnosis (being right) is our first concern and commitment." The other was his conviction that medicine, especially academic medicine, rests upon *humane scholarship*, which he defined in Buber's terms as concern for justice, compassion, and respect for scholarship. Instead of the traditional three-legged stool of education, research, and patient care, Papper proposed the three legs as education, research, and community, supporting a center of "people health," or care that takes into account the physical, emotional, social, and spiritual aspects of our being.

REFERENCE

1. Papper S: *Thirty-five Years in the Tower.* Boston/Toronto: Little, Brown and Company; 1985.

Connecticut Medicine 1999; 63(11):695–6

Section 4—Growing Old

The long habit of living indisposeth us for dying.

Thomas Browne (1605–1682)

Men do not quit playing because they grow old; they grow old because they quit playing.

Oliver Wendell Holmes (1809–1894)

The Last of Life, for Which the First was Made[1]

LAST month a group of aging physicians (seventh to the ninth decade) fell into—can you believe it?—the subject of aging. Being in a mildly depressed mood, I declared aging to be a disease of sorts, uncomfortable sometimes, only rarely malicious. A geriatrician in the crowd challenged me, as he should, on the use of the word "disease" and recalled John Rowe's and Robert Kahn's description of successful aging.[2] I argued that aging was more often defined by pathology all over the place, else why do we produce geriatricians rather than just gerontologists? We then fell randomly to describing our own various disorders and infirmities. As one of the crowd observed, "When someone asks me how I am, I say fine, but don't ask for details."

But, of course, the geriatrician was quite right. Aging is a natural condition of wearing out that comes ultimately and mercifully to an end, thanks to some watchful genes whose job it is to see to it that no tissues live forever, except, of course, germ cells. Heaven help us if we find some way of tampering with that ancient genetic sequence, replacing the lethal gene, upsetting the plan. [The physician and medical historian] Logan Clendening, speaking of nature's scheme for universal mortality, declared, "After having blundered on life, to have conceived of death was a real stroke of genius."

The geriatrician, warming to the prospect of widespread successful aging—absent accident, disease, immoderate habits, or suicide—rejoiced in the prospect of life spans of 120 years or more becoming commonplace. Not in the genes, I fervently hoped, not like the fruit flies! My uncharitable thoughts, prudently unspoken, were of the Four Horsemen of the Apocalypse: war, famine, pestilence, and death! Mess around with that fourth horseman, I thought, take him down, and the other three will come charging out of the stables to sustain him. Lewis Thomas had it right: in any complex system, "Intervening is a way of causing trouble."

But finding ways to prevent or reverse the major diseases of old age—dementia, heart disease, stroke, cancer, arthritis, chronic respiratory diseases, depression, and querulousness—may optimistically be anticipated during this first half century of the new millennium, sometime in the lifetimes of our grandchildren. Successful aging need not necessarily mean longer aging, but rather that more of us might live out our normal, mostly genetically determined, and relatively disease-free lifespans, which may be 70 years or

100 years, but rarely more. Surely by then most of us will have finished our work, ready, in Kipling's words, to "lie down for an eon or two."

I believe that all of us aging physicians were agreed that sometime after 70 years or so, we should avoid our colleagues' ministrations except when we require relief from pain, or when we are quite sure that our most recent disability may easily be remedied, or when we have some unfinished work that will require more time. In short, we should set limits to medical intrusions, as the medical ethicist, Daniel Callahan, advised. Another good physician friend, now at the end of his ninth decade, used to begin his talks to lay audiences by reminding them that "Mortality is 100%."

Contrast death in the 21st-century intensive-care unit with Emily Dickinson's metaphorical verses in "The Chariot," a poem that the literary critic Allen Tate called "one of the greatest in the English language":

> Because I could not stop for death,
> He kindly stopped for me;
> The carriage held but just ourselves
> And immortality.
>
> We slowly drove, he knew no haste,
> And I had put away
> My labor, and my leisure too,
> For his civility....

Finally, it is hard to abandon these thoughts without stopping to reread Cicero's *De senectute*. When I do, which is not often, I usually find something new to remember:

> The best end to life is with mind unclouded and faculties unimpaired, when nature herself dissolves what she has put together. The right person to take a ship or house to pieces is its builder; and by that analogy nature, which constructs human beings so skilfully, is also best at their demolition.

REFERENCES

1. Browning R: *Rabbi Ben Ezra.* English Poetry III: From Tennyson to Whitman. The Harvard Classics; 1909–14
2. Rowe JW, Kahn RL: Human aging: Usual and successful. *Science* 1987; 237:143–9.

Connecticut Medicine 2001; 65(2):113–4

O Tempora, O Mores, et Alia

ALTHOUGH in recent months I saw the path inevitably leading to the gate, I became uneasy as I opened it; it was the gateway into my ninth decade. Knowing that half of those who live past their 80th year will be demented before attaining fourscore and ten brings terror renewed whenever a familiar name or word is forgotten. One recalls Shakespeare's lines, or rather Jaques's, from *As You Like It*, as he ends his soliloquy that begins "All the world's a stage,"

> . . . Last scene of all,
> That ends this strange eventful history,
> In second childishness and mere oblivion,
> Sans teeth, sans eyes, sans taste, sans everything.

I have long had the habit of playing with dates; for example, taking my age and flipping the years backward through time beginning with my birth year. Someone born in 1842 would have been 80 when I was born in 1922. In 1842 Crawford Long removed a cyst from the neck of a patient, using ether to render him insensitive to pain. In 1844 Samuel Morse transmitted a telegraph message between Washington and Baltimore. In 1848 Karl Marx and Friedrich Engels published the *Communist Manifesto*. John Tyler was president, having succeeded William Henry Harrison in 1841. America would fight four wars during the 80 years before 1922, and four since.

In 80 years from now my children and grandchildren will be long gone, and my great-grandson, supposing we have not demolished the place, will be 80!

Those of us turning 80 this year will have lived though more than one third of the history of the Republic. And bits of oral history, mostly legend, learned from grandparents who had heard the stories from their grandparents, would span the entire 226 years since 1776.

These conceits must be common among the elderly; I have friends, otherwise quite lucid, who engage in similar light-headed daydreams. One has but to imagine himself an electron moving backward through time, and, for a short while, is a positron!

More real than these fanciful notions, though, is the growing sense that I am a stranger in a strange land. The world around me is no longer the world that formed my views of life. I read my newspapers and news magazines more quickly, even impatiently. They seem to carry less and less that interests me, except for the weather and the obituaries. They mostly report events, people, and politics that I find either irrelevant or unsavory. Even the funnies seem more often unfunny, their humor quite beyond me.

I have come to believe that much of this results from my relative indifference to the electronic revolution. My wife and I do not have email, do not have access to the web, nor are we hooked up to cable television. My younger friends are astonished; the subject comes up when they ask for my email address. When I say that I am blessed neither with email nor access to the web, they seem offended, as though I thought their ways frivolous. I do have a cell phone, but only to be available to my wife who is partially disabled. And it reassures me that I have indeed entered this third millennium, or at least am a tourist here.

My days are filled with spending time with my closest friend, my wife of 59 years, and with family, friends, caring for two dachshunds, and reading. Knowing that when we turn 80, like it or not, our future is not what it was at 65, I have determined to finish reading, or rereading, Shakespeare's plays and sonnets, Dante's *Divine Comedy,* Charles Dickens's and Henry James's novels, as much of Goethe as my inadequate German will bear, improving my Latin by reading the *Vulgate New Testament*, and learning as much as I can of quantum mechanics and its history. This last has become a fascination, or perhaps a mere fancy. It cannot last, I can't manage the math, but its history belongs largely to the world I have known, and the shadow world I dream about.

Connecticut Medicine 2002; 66(3):175

Geriatrics: Defining a New Specialty

> In as much as I no longer cling so hard to the good things of life when I begin to lose the use and pleasure of them, I come to view death with much less frightened eyes.
>
> *Montaigne (1533–1592)*[1]

IN geriatrics we have seen the birth and growth of a major medical specialty that defines itself in part by the age of its patients. Like its analogue pediatrics, whose practitioners in the early decades of this century declared their patients to be more than little adults, the protagonists of geriatrics argue with justification that their patients are not simply older adults. Moreover, just as infant feeding is hardly the province of the internist, so urinary incontinence may be brushed aside by the generalist as one of those inconveniences old men and women must endure. In but a score of years the small company of geriatricians has acquired new information about old problems that before had been accepted as inevitable, intractable accompaniments of aging. Furthermore, they have, like pediatricians, helped to shape public policy in support of their patients. They have defined and justified a body of knowledge that cuts across and enhances almost all of the older specialties, and have made long-term care a worthy academic discipline:

> Withering is nature's preparation for death, for the one who dies and for those who look upon him. We may wish to flee from it, perhaps, or seek to cover it over, but we must be cognizant of the costs of doing so.[2]

Because all of us have known octogenarians in full possession of their powers, we should have questioned our predilection for labeling illnesses that occur after Medicare as simply manifestations of senility. Kindly, most of us have said more than once, "Remember, you're not as young as you once were!" Or irritably, "What do you expect at your age?" Doctors, because they pass their days among the sick come to exaggerate their numbers, and, because many of the sick are old, come to believe that most elderly are frail, sick, and demented. I often forgot that my uncle, who lived in excellent health past 90, survived being gored by a bull at 92, and decided to give up smoking for good while recovering from the surgery to repair his small bowel. Last summer a close friend, age 87, fell off a roof, fractured his pelvis and three ribs, and was back working in two weeks. Everett Koop, then surgeon general, described a meeting with his old surgical chief, Jonathan Rhoads, by then 81, who declared he was fine, but that his practice was "falling off a little bit."[3] Heinrich Schütz, the early baroque composer, wrote his "Christmas Oratorio" at age 80 and Giovanni Battista Morgagni published his great work on anatomic pathology, *De sedibus et causis morborum*, when he was 79.

Yet there are diseases and disabilities that are frequent in old age, and some that are peculiar to the elderly. To deny that aging changes organs and tissues, diminishes physiologic functions, and that withering goes on inexorably to death, is to deny mortality and the benign order of nature. Too much busy intervening in this process will exact costs that we should never incur, yet our expensive, ingenious, specialist-driven technology is pushing us to do just that.

But geriatrics is not about such things; is not, if I understand it, seeking to extend our life span beyond that devised by nature. Rather, geriatrics seeks to learn the ways of successful aging and to offer beneficent, simple, and reliable guides along the road that most of us, willy-nilly, will travel. The voice that is missing, however, is the voice of the elderly themselves. With their advocacy of autonomy, the geriatricians will help them regain it, and then listen to all that those of them who "view death with much less frightened eyes" may have to say about growing old!

REFERENCES

1. From Montaigne, "That to Philosophize Is to Learn to Die," quoted in Kass LR: *Toward a More Natural Science.* New York: The Free Press; 1985:307.
2. Kass LR: Mortality and morality: The virtues of finitude. In: *Toward a More Natural Science.* New York: The Free Press; 1985:299–317.
3. Koop CE: *Koop: The Memoirs of America's Family Doctor*. New York: Random House; 1991:63.

Connecticut Medicine 1993; 57(5):353

Health-Care Reform and Long-Term Care

LONG-TERM care insurance should be one of the components of health-care reform, but it may not even be close to the top of the priority list. Its costs are too high for more than a small percentage of the population, and could be reduced only by spreading premium payments, like Social Security, over a long period of time. But the most serious problem, according to Anne R. Somers, ". . . is a total 'disconnect' between the [long-term care] insurance policy and the provision of care, leaving even the expensively insured patient unprotected as to the quality of the covered services."[1]

A definitive history of the care of the elderly in America has yet to be written; the specialty of geriatrics is about where pediatrics was in the first decades of this century. The nursing home has evolved remarkably during my half-century in medicine, but its quality has remained spotty, probably because most long-term care ventures began as businesses driven by profit rather than as community services. Tougher standards have improved quality, or at least the appearance of quality, but in the long run profitability is a poor objective when a community seeks to care for its dependent elderly members. Standards can be skirted, and regulation is uneven and expensive; the only assurance of quality is conscientious, dedicated administration, a committed, attentive board, and an intelligent, skillful, compassionate professional staff. Business-like, but not a business!

From a warehouse for the chronically ill, impoverished, or impaired elderly to a lively community working to meet the needs and fulfill the reasonable wants of older women and men is a long, but not impossible, step. Continuing care retirement communities (CCRCs) are one answer, but not everyone's solution, and still too costly for most. From assisted home living to hospice, with all levels in between, ought to be the objective of any long-term care plan, supported by some form of long-term care insurance.

> But regulation and social policy is often inconsistent and sometimes makes good care harder rather than easier to provide—in part because we have not, as a society, truly worked out a moral vision and a set of aspirations for what we want nursing homes to be.[2]

This is hardly surprising; we have had the problem for little more than 50 years. When most retirees lived only six months or a year after retirement; when families stayed put, and half of them lived in small towns or on the farm; when most wives and mothers were at home all day, helped by one or two of the older daughters, care for grandmother was an expected part of family life. Few worried about a moral vision of what nursing homes should be. There were county old people's homes for those few elderly who had outlived their families, or whose children had moved away, perhaps too poor or too shiftless to care for them. These were government homes, now comprising only 5% of the 19,000 nursing homes in the United States.[2]

Society rarely works out a clear moral vision of institutions or anything else, but thoughtful, far-seeing individuals dream dreams and build models, some of which work, and the successful models become society's vision and are then replicated. We are in that process now; CCRCs are one model. There are others: nursing homes that provide for assisted living, home care, day care, sheltered living, skilled nursing care that is but little removed from hospital care, especially now that hospitals have turned into vast intensive care units that are quite inappropriate for most geriatric care, and finally care at the very end of life, hospice care. They have yet, for the most part, failed to evolve from institutions to moral communities whose citizens help to run the place, but the best ones know that and are working on it.

The specialty of geriatrics and the institutions that we call nursing homes, although some are much more than that, are just beginning their history. To grow and mature to meet society's needs they will require close attention from those who are trying to figure out how to nurture our health-care system in the 21st century.

REFERENCES

1. Somers AR: "Lifecare": A viable option for long-term care for the elderly. *J Am Geriatr Soc* 1993; 41:188–91.
2. Collopy B, Boyle P, Jennings B: New directions in nursing home ethics. *Hastings Cent Rep* (Special Supplement) March/April 1991; 21(2):1–15.

Connecticut Medicine 1993; 57(4):245

Section 5—Facing Our Mortality: Death and Dying

Any man's death diminishes me, because I am involved in mankind; and therefore never send to know for whom the bell tolls; it tolls for thee.

John Donne (1572–1631)

I want death to find me planting my cabbages.

Michel Eyquem de Montaigne (1533–1592)

No Easy Matter

> With what strift and pains we come into the World we remember not; but 'tis commonly found no easy matter to get out of it.[1]

THOMAS Browne (1605–1682) could hardly have imagined how cleverly we would "exasperate the ways of Death"[1] in the late 20th century; but that his 17th-century mind would have been as perplexed as ours is doubtful.

I recall hearing an English physician describe the principles of hospice care 12 years ago or so. "You must reach a point," he said, "when you quite consciously and deliberately decide, with the patient, to do nothing more to treat the disease, but rather that you will bend all your efforts to relieve the patient's pain, physical, mental, spiritual, and economic." To stop wrestling with death, to quit the post seemed to me, at first hearing, to violate the most sacred principle of medicine. Weren't we winning the battle against infectious diseases, maybe against cancer, quite clearly against heart disease? Who could know what cure tomorrow would bring, how could anyone give up? *Dum spiro, spero* [while I breathe, I hope] we had learned in 10th-grade Latin, and now understood what it meant!

The old hospice idea was reborn among nurses and their patients; they knew, often better than we doctors did, when the jig was up; they would benignly tolerate our barely effective efforts to manipulate electrolytes, juggle antibiotics (there were only three or four), add ascorbic acid or aminophylline to mercuhydrin, and order liters of protein hydrolysate. We could do all that unobtrusively, fighting the battle, while they were attending to the dying patient's comfort, changing his position, rubbing his back, keeping his mouth moist and the bed dry, keeping him company. We did little to interfere.

But then in the space of two decades it has all changed; our machines can prolong dying for days, weeks, months, even years. Technology has a way of becoming its own end. In Dr. Forman's essay, which I mentioned last month, describing Mr. Rosen's long, painful death (*New York Times*, 12 April 1988) we see the image of late 20th-century medicine that our 21st-century descendants will surely wonder at:

> Highly trained technically, we often lack the emotional grounding to confront the pain of inevitable death. While medical care is implemented

reflexively out of both legal and philosophical obligations, a sense of guilt and regret exists in many of us who prolong such a grim course.

Our defense is rarely medical or philosophic; more often we are frightened of the legal swamp, "the myth of the incarcerated physician and the specter of the large civil verdict haunt our nation's intensive care units."[2] Yet when hospitals and physicians have honored their patients' requests, or the requests of surrogates, there has never been a successful action against them.

Early in the last century when Benjamin Rush and others were advocating heroic bleeding and purging, many of their patients turned to the homeopaths, hydrotherapists, Thomsonians, and Christian Scientists. It would be oversimplifying to conclude that heroic medicine declined only because the public was taking up with the sectarians, but that was not without its effect. It will take public pressure again to make us temperate in the use of modern heroic therapy, to stop probing, testing, intubating, monitoring, treating, resuscitating when there is no point. Our patients, in increasing numbers, will encourage us to talk to them first, rather than to whisper in corridors with their families, about how their last illnesses are to be managed. Those advance directives are entirely theirs to make while their minds are clear enough, and our job is to help them to understand what the future will be like, to employ our skill in prognosis: "I hold that it is an excellent thing for a patient to practice forecasting."[3]

A senior surgeon recently expressed to me his perplexity over this matter ever being a problem; "I can't imagine," he said, "not *always* discussing these things with both patient and family."

REFERENCES

1. Browne Sir Thomas: *Christian Morals*, part II, sect. XIII; also in *Letter to a Friend,* sect. V.
2. Armstrong PW, Colen BD: From Quinlan to Jobes: The courts and the PVS patient. *Hastings Cent Rep* 1988;18(February/March):37–40.
3. Hippocrates, *Prognostic*, 1.

Connecticut Medicine 1988; 52(8):505

Sustainable Progress: Is It Possible?

MORE often than not a nonmedical friend, hoping to express his admiration for our profession, will comment on the wonders of modern medicine, especially how they have increased our life expectancy. Most often I briefly agree but change the subject. It seems captious, even disloyal, to remark that clean food, refrigeration, and good plumbing may have contributed even more. Or to observe that half the population over 85 are demented, or that the major determinants of longer life expectancy for which scientific medicine may claim major credit, are the decline in infant and maternal mortality and the prevention of serious childhood diseases. The old-old are no older than they used to be. My great-grandmother was born in 1835 and died in 1935. Only one of my more recent forebears lived 86 years; for the others the average age at death was 63.

Recently several friends, after receiving the bad news that they had cancer, have refused chemotherapy and insisted that no further tests or procedures be done. "Just keep me as pain-free as possible—and out of the hospital!" You may recall the stir a decade or so ago when Daniel Callahan's book appeared, *Setting Limits: Medical Goals in an Aging Society*. Some first-rate geriatricians were appalled. One remarked to me that "Dan should have known better." But Callahan continued his theme in *The Tyranny of Survival: And Other Pathologies of Civilized Life* and in *False Hopes: Why America's Quest for Perfect Health Is a Recipe for Failure.* Some years ago, the philosopher Sidney Hook wrote, "The fear of death, the desire to survive at any cost or price in human degradation, has been the greatest ally of tyranny, past or present."

Sometimes, when my wife and I discuss these cheerful matters, one of us will quote Frederick the Great's words shouted to his troops who had dared slow their march, hesitating in fear before a battle. "Hunde, wollt ihr ewig leben?" (Dogs, do you want to live forever?)

"It is, at first glance, curious that dissatisfaction with medicine in America is at its most vociferous just at a time when doctors have at their disposal the most powerful technology the world has yet seen." Leon Eisenberg, professor of psychiatry at Harvard, wrote that 27 years ago! The cost of medical care was then 118 billion dollars or 8.3 per cent of the GNP. Allowing for inflation we are now spending about 2.5 times that amount, and we have almost two times as many physicians per hundred thousand—about 250, or one for every 400 persons. Judging from comments by both colleagues and neighbors, a high and increasing level of dissatisfaction with the commercialized medical-technological complex is rampant. Costs per person are now over 3,500 dollars annually, or 14,000 dollars for a family of four. Some studies have shown that more medical interventions, more tests, more tampering, increase the risk of harm to patients, in keeping with the law of diminishing returns.[1]

Callahan urged that at some point in our lives, perhaps in our eighth or ninth decade, we should set limits and determine, as best we can, our way to escape a wild death in the ICU [intensive care unit], pummeled by the halfway technologies of modern medicine. Too often, the technological imperative overpowers the good judgment of the physician, and goes far beyond the will of the patient.

Perhaps the sanest and most admirable innovation in medical care during the past 30 years has been a reintroduction of the concept of hospice, once a way station for tired travelers, for the sick, a place of peace, often maintained by a religious order.

Modern medicine and its machines have set a barrier between physician and patient, eliminating, or so it is thought, the need to talk to or hear from the suffering (*patiens*) or troubled person. Fifteen-minute visits between strangers hardly represents for the physician the culmination of eight years of education, or the patient's hope for care. But why worry? The machines will make the diagnosis and there is a drug or procedure for every problem. This amazing progress has come at great and increasing costs to all of us. Callahan made the startling recommendation of a "steady-state" medicine, a sustainable medicine. "The dream of modern medicine," he wrote, "—that life, death, and illness can be scientifically dominated and pacified—will be one of the most difficult to give up." And, one might add, especially because it has been so expensive, and therefore so profitable to so many—almost like illicit drugs.

But there is a light, or rather a lamp, now visible at the end of the road. The hospice movement, begun in recent times by Dame Cecily Saunders at St. Christopher's Hospital in London, took root on this side of the Atlantic in Connecticut about 30 years ago. It is indeed a steady-state sustainable medicine, at least for those nearing the end of their lives, as well as for their loved ones. No high technology, just the kind of care once described for all of medicine in the Middle Ages: to cure sometimes, to relieve often, to comfort always.

Hospice care is sometimes poorly imitated, mostly because it may be attempted by hospitals that are still in the business of technologically-driven "health care." The ideals and motivations are quite different; the two, hospices and hospitals, play by different rules. A hospice could never be "for-profit," and, of course, no hospital should be either, but they are driven by wondrous machines and the market-place to make for-profit-like decisions. Hospices do their skillful, quiet, devoted, and humane work quite like their kind 500 years ago. Theirs is nonprogressive, steady-state progress! Again, Callahan wrote:

> By its tacit implication that in the quest for health lies, perhaps, the secret of the meaning of life, modern medicine has misled people into thinking that the ills of the flesh, and mortality itself, are not to be understood and integrated into a balanced view of life but simply to be fought and resisted.

"Yet medicine, itself," he added, "is not necessarily at fault for the strain of health-religiosity, or 'healthism.'. . . Rather by hitching itself uncritically to the hubris of modernism, it has created a whole range of incipient problems, but especially the desire for unlimited improvement, which are now fully expressed."

Last month, in *Connecticut Medicine*, Dr. James D. Duffy wrote: "While scientific materialism provides many useful tools for tinkering with human physiology, it provides no wisdom capable of directing the enormous potential we are unleashing."

The hospice idea was to provide care for the dying, for those who had agreed that no more was to be done than to provide care and comfort and relief from pain. The notion is growing that hospice-like care may also be provided to those whose lives have extended into their eighth and ninth decades, who know that they are playing out the final act of the drama of life, and who wish nothing further to be done medically except that which may relieve pain and provide comfort. No more tests, EKGs, and scans, for they, using Callahan's words, have set limits!

G. K. Chesterton (1874–1936) wrote some lines on separate occasions using the image of the hospice, the inn at the end of the road:

> My friends we will not go again or ape an ancient rage,
> Or stretch the folly of our youth to be the shame of age,
> But walk with clearer eyes and ears this path that wandereth,
> And see undrugg'd in evening light the decent inn of death;

For there is good news yet to hear and fine things to be seen,
Before we go to Paradise by way of Kensal Green.

from *The Rolling English Road*

The inn does not point to the road; the road points to the inn. And all roads point at last to an ultimate inn, where we shall meet Dickens and all his characters: and when we drink again it shall be from the great flagons in the tavern at the end of the world.

from *Charles Dickens: The Last of the Great Men*

REFERENCE

1. Fisher ES, Welch HG: Avoiding the unintended consequences of growth in medical care: How more might be worse? *JAMA* 1999; 281:446–51.

Connecticut Medicine 2002; 66(12):769–70

Requiescas, Sophie

Thou shalt not kill; but need'st not strive
Officiously to keep alive.
Arthur Hugh Clough (1819–1861)

WE have owned dachshunds for over 50 years, usually, but not always, a pair. The female member of our last pair died in January. She had had more than her just share of illness and disability: Lyme disease, followed by Lyme arthritis, hypothyroidism caused by her inability to convert T4 to the active hormone T3, intestinal obstruction initiated by a chicken bone, which she should have known better than to swallow, spinal disc problems, an ulnar fracture, deafness, and periodontal disease. I would not want any of our other dogs to think that she may have been our favorite; every dog at one time or another is a favorite!

She was a beautiful, red, long-haired little thing, never weighing more than nine and half pounds. Dachshunde (the proper plural!) are long-lived dogs; most of ours reached 17 or 18 years. We had named her in a fit of fancy Sophie Charlotte von Hannover, after the daughter of the Electress Sophie of Hannover, who later became Electress of Brandenburg, and finally Queen of Prussia. Her brother was the first Hanoverian King of England, George I, who was rather dull, but Sophie Charlotte and her mother were known as "die kluge Frauen" (the bright women) because of their close friendship with and support for the philosopher Leibniz. Of course, our Sophie Charlotte was also "eine kluge Frau," a brilliant lady!

Her death came quickly on a Sunday following her breakfast and a shower with me. She was suddenly unable to stand as I was drying her, seemed drowsy and shortly became unresponsive. Her temperature was 90° (normal for a dog is well over 100°). I wrapped her in a blanket and held her in my rocker. In an hour or two she was dead. I had resisted family suggestions to take her to an emergency vet; I knew she was dying and I wanted her to die at home. My regular veterinary physician whom I consulted the next day thought she either had had a sudden arrhythmia or a cerebral bleed, and he agreed that death at home in my arms was far better than alone in a cage in his or any veterinary hospital.

Sophie had lived the last seven of her 14 years after my retirement, so I was with her, and our younger male dachshund, Franz Josef, every day, most of the day. They slept with my wife and me, almost never moving. We feel alone and low spirited without her. The cold winter makes it worse. Dogs are warm bedfellows.

The intensity of grief following the unexpected death of our dog, especially one so close, surprised me. Yet we had often said to one another that we could hardly imagine our lives with either one of them gone.

In his book, *Man on His Nature*, Charles Sherrington wrote:

> That a cell-aggregate, such as our friend the dog, is in his doings an integrated individual, a system of acts—for that is all we really know him as—and does what he does, we tend to account for by saying he is unified by his mind. As he walks beside us with his ways, and the thoughts we imagine in him, what is the relative contribution to him, as an individual, made by his doings with and those without his mind? We cannot answer fully—

I found myself asking, where now is *her* mind, a mind that I was quite certain knew more about me than I about her, who sensed moods, understood actions even though she heard no words, had loves, and likes, as well as intense dislikes. Her mind and body together gave her, as they give us, a unique *persona*. Mind is a kind of organized energy; with cell death, the organization is gone. I liken it to a tray of six-point type that the printer's devil has just dropped—organization has become a meaningless jumble, yet it remains intact somewhere—on the author's desk or in his word processor, not lost.

Many of us, perhaps most, have accepted, in one guise or another, Pascal's wager [Blaise Pascal, French philospher and mathematician, 1623–1662] rather than holding with certainty to an unverifiable belief. The nothingness of death, like a black hole, is quite beyond our event horizon. Yet I find comfort in recalling Matthew 10:29, "Are not two sparrows sold for a penny? And not one of them will fall to the ground without your Father."

Connecticut Medicine 2003; 67(2):121

Drosophila and Donne's Shroud

SEVERAL weeks ago *Science* published a brief observation regarding *Drosophila* suggesting that these remarkable flies anticipate death by lying on their backs from time to time several days before the end of their short lives, the position they, like most flies, assume when their vital spirits fail them! Are they reminding their fellows, please, when my time comes, do not resuscitate?

The image of John Donne (1572–1631) came immediately to mind. I read somewhere that he had had a coffin placed in his bed chamber, and, after wrapping himself in a shroud, proceeded to lie down in it. When he was dean of St. Paul's in London, he had a funeral statue made of himself wrapped in his shroud. That strange sculpture, I'm told, still stands in the cathedral. I doubt that Donne is now permitted in public high schools; he was so politically incorrect! But I do recall reading, in 11th-grade English lit, these lines from which Ernest Hemingway had taken the title for his 1940 novel:

> No man is an Iland intire of itself; every man is a peece of the Continent, a part of the maine; if a Clod be washed away by the Sea, Europe is the lesse, as well as if a Promontorie were, as well as if a Manor of thy friends or of thine own were. Any man's death diminishes me, because I am involved in Mankind. And therefore never send to know for whom the bell tolls. It tolls for thee.

Perhaps because of his obsession with death, as well as his "misspent learning and excessive ingenuity," he remained controversial, even maddening, among critics of English poetry. Harold Bloom omits him without comment from his *Western Canon*. Sir Edmund Gosse, in my 1952 *Encyclopedia Britannica*, writes, "The influence of Donne upon the literature of England was singularly wide and deep, although almost wholly malign." C. S. Lewis in his *English Literature in the Sixteenth Century* [The Clarendon Press, Oxford; 1954], condemns Donne for writing "under the influence of the old blunder which connected *satira* with *satyros*[1] and concluded that the one should be as shaggy and 'salvage' as the other. . . . In Donne if any simile or allusion leads us away from the main theme, it leads us only to other objects of contempt and disgust—to coffins, 'itchie lust,' catamites, dearth, pestilence, a condemned wretch 'at Barre,' vomit, excrement, botches, pox, 'carted whores'" [pp. 469–70].

Death had haunted Donne from youth. He had frequent thoughts of suicide. "Methinks I have the keys of my prison in my own hand, and no remedy presents itself so soon to my heart as mine own sword." He considered martyrdom as a way to achieve both death and blessedness. His last sermon, published after his death at age 58, was titled *Death's Duel*. Gosse declared his terminal illness "a malarial form of recurrent quinsy acting upon an extremely neurotic system" (malaria?). He commissioned a painting of himself wrapped in his shroud and kept it at his bedside, "his hourly object until his death."

Extremely neurotic, perhaps. Yet as with most psychopathology, an exaggeration of the normal. His life had been hard, and, like St. Augustine's, in his youth a bit raunchy. He eloped with a nobleman's niece, Anne More, was arrested, imprisoned, wrote to his mother, "John Donne—Ann Donne—Undone." Donne abandoned his Catholic faith at 42, took Anglican orders, was appointed dean of St. Paul's London, and was to have been made bishop in 1630 but for his illness; he died in 1631 at age 58.

But recurring thoughts of death, I am certain, need not always indicate clinical depression, anymore with us than with *Drosophila*. As children and adolescents we seem immortal. An occasional schoolmate's death by accident is unsettling, but the dark, teary mood quickly passes. In my parents' days, I recall hearing at cocktail parties that "life begins at 40, after all!, ha, ha, ha." Mortality was becoming, with the death of sister or parent from cancer, an uncomfortable image, yet still remote. My father, approaching 50, at times unbidden, recalled and recited his favorite lines from Tennyson:

> Sunset and evening star,
> And one clear call for me!
> And may there be no moaning of the bar,
> When I put out to sea.

He died at 52, six years younger than Donne's age at death. I never in my life saw him depressed.

At age 60 more contemporaries, not many, begin to fall away. By the late 70s, early 80s, hardly a month goes by without an old friend or sibling or cousin going the way of all flesh. Osler wrote in a letter, "—and in one's 71st year the harbor is not far off. And such a happy voyage! & such dear companions all the way! It would be nice to find Isaac[2] there, with his friend Izaak Walton & others, but who knows." Perhaps he was thinking of Donne's lines:

> Death be not proud, though some have called thee
> Mighty and dreadful, for thou art not so; . . . .
> One short sleep past, we wake eternally,
> And death shall be no more; Death, thou shalt die.

Stewart Hamilton once told me, early in my 71st year, that I would perceive more changes in myself in the coming 10 years than in any previous decade, except perhaps for the second! He was right! By the beginning of the ninth decade, one begins to feel a stranger in an increasingly strange and not always pleasant land. The newspaper reports events that seem mostly irrelevant. I can finish the morning paper in 15 minutes, including the comics, many of which I no longer understand nor find funny. Even the weekly newsmagazine seems not only irrelevant, but tiresome, even offensive. I'm eager to get back to Dickens, Shakespeare, Dante, T.S. Eliot, or perhaps Willa Cather or Graham Greene. George Steiner caught the feeling in the opening pages of his *Grammars of Creation*:

> Nevertheless, there is, I think, in the climate or spirit at the end of the 20th-century, a core tiredness. The inward chronometry, the contracts with time which so largely determine our consciousness, point to late afternoon in ways that are ontological—this is to say, of the essence, of the fabric of being. We are, or feel ourselves to be, latecomers. The dishes are being cleared. "Time, ladies and gents, time." Valediction is in the air.

Perhaps it is the voice of a man growing old, or the mood of our time after finishing with a terrifying century. Loren Eisely in his life of Francis Bacon, *The Man Who Saw Through Time,* wrote of those 16th-century years,

> The smell of an autumnal decay pervaded the entire Elizabethan world. Over all that age . . . there was a subdued feeling in men's hearts that the sands in the hourglass were well-nigh run. It was autumn, late autumn, and God was weary of the play.

It seems to me that these moods must come mostly toward the ends of our lives, after our living memory has retained, for many of us, bits and pieces of four, maybe even five generations. Such moods are not depressing, but rather, restful. We've changed too often and anticipate no more turnings; there comes a time, T. S. Eliot wrote [in *Ash Wednesday*], not to turn again:

> Because I do not hope to turn again
> Because I do not hope
> Because I do not hope to turn
> Desiring this man's gift and that man's scope
> I no longer strive to strive towards such things
> (Why should the aged eagle stretch its wings?)
> Why should I mourn
> The vanished power of the usual reign?

REFERENCES

1. *Satira*, Latin, a literary form, satire; *Satyros*, Ζατυροζ, Greek, a satyr, a lewd, goatish fellow.
2. Isaac was Osler's nickname for his son Revere, who had fallen at Ypres in August 1917. He was called Isaac by his father because he was such an ardent fisherman, like Izaak Walton (1593–1683).

Connecticut Medicine 2002; 66(10):629–30

When the Time for Heroics Has Passed

> Many have studied to exasperate the ways of Death, but fewer hours have been spent to soften that necessity.
>
> *Thomas Browne (1605–1682)*

PHYSICIANS have never quite known how to behave at the bedside of their dying patients. It may even have been harder 30 years ago before our amazing life-extending (or dying-extending) technologies were available to keep us busy. I knew a distinguished endocrinologist who, when his patient took her last breath as he stood by, seemed embarrassed, crossed himself, bowed slightly, and backed out of the room. Sometimes in those far off days we would call for an epinephrin-filled syringe with a long needle and aim it at the precordium, empty it, and wait. In my experience nothing ever happened, but we could leave feeling that we had done our best.

Now hospital deaths are often wild, a confusion of unfeeling, but well-meaning, noisy busyness in the ICU, nurses and housestaff standing by or manipulating tubes, defibrillators, respirators, or just watching the monitor as someone forcibly and rhythmically compresses the chest. Hardly the *euthanasia*, the peaceful departure, the good death that the ancients wished for themselves and their families. Daniel Callahan wrote of the "wild death," earlier described by Philippe Ariès, and now so common in our hospitals:

> It is wild not simply because it is out of control and terrorizing in its modern incarnation, but also because, in the name of combating mortality, it has managed simultaneously to subvert the institution of medicine, which cannot overcome mortality, and the morality of human decisions about life and death, which should not have to bear the burden of omni-responsibility.[1(99)]

Callahan hardly intended to deny anyone the right to choose the wild death, ". . . technological brinkmanship without restraint, aiming to go as far as medical aggressiveness will allow," but that he should know and be prepared to accept "risking a terrible death—a risk for himself but also for those who must care for him."[1(206)]

In discussions with older men and women, those mostly well beyond the Psalmist's three score and ten, I have found an almost universal fear—even terror—that instead of that peaceful death that nature so often provides, they will be pummeled by EMTs, delivered to the ER, and then rolled away to the ICU with absolutely no choice in the matter, and spouses or children powerless, or not aggressive enough, to intercede. Over and over I hear of living wills ignored, especially when they could not be produced on the spot. One elderly man thought he might have DNR [do not resuscitate] tattooed on his forehead! More than this, many are concerned that in the helplessness of their final illness they will be subtly urged by well-meaning families and physicians to have just one more round of chemotherapy or radiation, or will be cheated out of a quiet death from pneumonia. I recall a wife and her two sons, both ministers, blocking the hospital room doorway of her husband and their father, near death from leukemia, for whose pneumonia a resident had, not inappropriately, ordered antibiotics to be given. They won the standoff, but only because they were able to reach the patient's physician and friend by phone. The patient died a peaceful death 24 hours later, and the resident sulked.

Leon Kass writes that our urge to medicalize death is *hubris* and reminds us of the tragic fate awaiting those who succumb to this all-too-human fault. "We do not understand that the project for the conquest of death leads only to dehumanization, that any attempt to gain the tree of life by means of the tree of knowledge leads inevitably to the hemlock. . . ." and that "the victors live long enough to finish life demented and without choice." He concludes:

> The present crisis that leads some to press for active euthanasia is really an opportunity to learn the limits of the medicalization of life and death and to recover an appreciation of living with and against mortality. It is an opportunity to remember and affirm that there remains a residual human wholeness—however precarious—that can be cared for in the face of incurable and terminal illness. Should we cave in, should we choose to become technical dispensers of death, we will not only be abandoning our loved ones and our duty to care; we will exacerbate the worst tendencies of modern life, embracing technicism and so-called humaneness where encouragement and humanity are both required and sorely lacking.[2(141)]

Over 170 years ago, a medical student at Göttingen by the name of Carl Friedrich Heinrich Marx wrote his doctoral thesis, *De euthanasia medica*, "Medical Euthanasia,"[3] by which he meant, not the active euthanasia, the killing that many are demanding as an alternative to a wild medicalized death, but rather the passive good death, the peaceful death of skillful palliation that today defines hospice care. Almost two centuries ago this newly minted *Med. et Chir. Dr.* from his ancient university in Brunswick reminded his fellow academics of that "great Englishman," Francis Bacon, who had written 200 years earlier urging physicians "to stay with the patient after he is given up, . . ." and "to acquire the skill and to bestow the attention whereby the dying may pass more easily and quietly out of life."

Marx's recommendations were strikingly similar to the principles of hospice care today; he would have understood, as perhaps would Bacon, the notion of physician assisted living (PAL) during life's final exit. "Most physicians," he wrote, "once they see the expected result of their treatment to be wanting, . . . start to lose interest themselves." He even mentions a program at Heidelberg headed by a Professor Mai, and funded by Amalia, Duchess of Baden, that provided training to women attendants in caring for the sick and the terminally ill. Marx recommended that these caregivers be "considerate, watchful, quiet, clean, free of prejudice toward people, . . . and adhere to the doctor's orders with greatest obedience." He described the care of bedsores, and that the "doctor will with his own eyes repeatedly search for" them.

Marx asked, "What good will it do the incurable patient to apply dangerous and dubious therapeutic measures? The entire plan of treatment will here confine itself within 'symptomatic and palliative medication.'" He even reminded his physician colleagues to see that the patient's dry tongue and pharynx be moistened. He urged "soothing, soporific, sedative, analgesic" medicines, and noted that ". . . narcotics are of enormous help." But later he added the essential caveat, ". . . and least of all should he be *permitted* (italics mine), prompted either by other people's requests or by his own sense of mercy, to end the patient's pitiful condition by purposely and deliberately hastening death. How can it be permitted that he who is by law required to preserve life be the originator of, or partner in, its destruction?"

In Marx's brief thesis, written in 1826 upon his being admitted to the faculty at Göttingen, we can find all the principles of hospice care and of physician care at the end of life embodied in the PAL program. Nothing new here. But even he was not their originator; we find them not only in Bacon, but in the ancients—Pliny, Cicero, Seneca, the Bible. They are imbedded somehow in our nature, and even, as Lewis Thomas once suggested in nature itself: why else the endorphins? Concerning them he wrote, "If I had to design an ecosystem in which creatures had to live off each other and in which dying was an indispensable part of living, I could not think of a better way to manage."

But when endorphins are not enough for the kinds of nonviolent, prolonged deaths that we often produce and must endure, we have the means and the inherent mercy to ease the passage. We should pay more attention to the business of dying. My Harrison's *Principles of Internal Medicine* devotes

[only] one and one half pages out of 2,044 to this matter, but it does address the physician's role: "First of all, the patient must be given an opportunity to speak to his physician and to ask questions."

This is what the PAL program as a part of the advanced directive is all about. It frees patients who are prepared to plan for the inevitable event to consider the options, discuss them with their physicians and families, choose, and then say with Seneca: "I am ready for death, hence I may enjoy life."

REFERENCES

1. Callahan D: *The Troubled Dream of Life: Living with Mortality.* New York: Simon & Schuster; 1993.
2. Kass LR: Death with dignity and the sanctity of life. In: Kogan BS, ed: *A Time to Be Born and a Time to Die: The Ethics of Choice.* New York: Aldine de Gruyter; 1991:117–45.
3. Cane W: Medical euthanasia. A paper published in Latin in 1826, translated and reintroduced to the medical profession. *J Hist Med Allied Sci* 1952; 7:401–16.

Connecticut Medicine 1997; 61(12):803–4

How Much Life Extension Can We Stand?

> The days of our years are threescore years and ten; and if by reason of strength they be fourscore years, yet is their strength labour and sorrow; for it is soon cut off, and we fly away.
>
> *Psalm 90:10.*

IN 1993, for the first time in years, life expectancy fell in the United States, but the fall was tiny and could hardly be the beginning of a trend. Until relatively recently, life expectancy increased because of declining infant and childhood mortality. Now the increases are largely at the other end, with the over 85 crowd growing fast. Their numbers are expected to triple to almost nine million by 2030. By that year, when the oldest Boomers will be 84, the elderly, those over 65, will make up 20% of our population. According to one estimate, the 65-and-over group in 2040 will total 127.5 million, equal to the population of the entire country in the 1930s. Recently *Science* (July 5, 1996) devoted its news section to "Horizons on Aging," and painted anything but a cheering demographic picture, not only for the United States but for the entire planet. Implications for Medicare and Social Security, and their analogs in other developed nations, are frightening. Social democracies like Germany are already feeling generational hostility.

Research into the many factors making up the aging process: heredity, genetics, nutrition, stress, immune function, endocrine system malfunction, and changes in connective tissue, continue to be intellectually rewarding. Distinguished and prudent investigators, however, have more than once informally whispered that such research ought never to be funded! Or the results never accepted for publication or, if published, never put to use. Publicly such sentiments are rarely given voice, but there is among thoughtful bioscientists a kind of ethical unease, a primordial fear that too much knowledge may lead to too much power and ultimately to our undoing.

I recently reread some of the papers in an 18-year-old issue of *Daedalus* whose authors were distinguished leaders in that decade in the biological sciences, in technology, and in the history, ethics, and sociology of science. The Spring 1978 issue was called "Limits of Scientific Inquiry," and the editor felt the time was "propitious for a more objective inquiry" into a concept that would have been unthinkable 20, or even 10, years before.

Research on aging came in for more worried comment than most other endeavors. The year before (*Daedalus* Winter 1977) Daniel Callahan had asked, "If death can be forestalled, for how long and in what circumstances should it be?" Robert Sinsheimer listed three areas of research that he considered of dubious merit; one was research on the aging process: ". . . on a finite planet extended individual life must restrict the production of new individuals and that renewal which provides the vitality of our species." Robert S. Morison admitted that, dubious or not, such research is unlikely to be limited:

> The love of life is so thoroughly built into us that at first glance it seems impossible for any substantial fraction of the human race to want anything else but its dubious extension. . . .
>
> Our main point is that the very universality of appeal that makes life-extension so patently disruptive and amply justifies the concerns so far expressed, at the same time renders it immune from social control by limiting research on the aging process or banning the development of the consequent technologies.

Social control is an even more frightening concept now than it was 18 years ago. Getting permission for research from busybody committees or arrogant bureaucrats who know little about how science works evokes bad dreams of the Thought Police.

But what about cultural restraint? When Morison wrote those lines he was a visiting professor at M.I.T. and 72 years old. It seems to me that since 1978 there has been more openness about death and the preparation for death as the acceptable final chapter in life, due to arrive sometime during the decade or so after the psalmist's "three score and ten," or sooner if the burden of illness or pain should become too heavy to bear. Daniel Callahan's *Setting Limits* started us talking seriously about that. I hear more talk of restraint in using life-extending technologies when a full life has been lived. Perhaps I have listened to a nonrepresentative group of men and women, but they belong mostly to the crowd that sets the tone for society as whole; the idea of limits just might return to a culture used to thinking that death is an option.

Connecticut Medicine 1996; 60(8):501

I Will Give No Deadly Medicine to Anyone If Asked, Nor Suggest Any Such Counsel

Hippocratic Oath, Hippocrates (c. 460–377 B.C.)

THE matter of physician-assisted suicide, under discussion long before the Oath was composed, will not go away, and it will come to divide us just as the abortion issue has done. For those for whom abortion is murder there can be no middle ground, no compromise; for those who share the traditional, although often paradoxical, abhorrence of the Western world for suicide, there is rarely found justification for self-murder. Participating in abortion or suicide may be legal, may even become reimbursable under universal health insurance, providing income for the physician and product lines for the managed-care business, but for most, I suspect, will never feel comfortably ethical. Even for many of those who are intellectually convinced, there will linger a troubling feeling of dread in contemplating either act.

Richard Selzer in his book *Letters to a Young Doctor* tells the story of a man wasted by seven years of pancreatic cancer, and how wife, mother, and patient, no longer willing to endure more, beg the doctor for release.[1] Enough morphine to stop the pain must surely end the life of this 80-pound man, and his physician gives it, but he did not die. The story ends with this brief exchange between the doctor and the mother and the man's wife:

> "He didn't die," I say. "He won't . . . or can't." They are silent.
>
> "He isn't ready yet," I say.
>
> "He *is* ready, the old woman says. "You *ain't.*"

In this issue there is an essay, reprinted from *JAMA*, *A Conversation With My Mother*, by Dr. David M. Eddy of Jackson, Wyoming.[2] It is the story of his mother's final illness and his resolve to help her end her life. For a physician finally to enter upon this agonizing task of assisting in ending another's life he must, at the least, somehow "resolve any lingering conflicts and obtain the drugs . . ." His mother, after pneumonia fails, asks about another way: could she stop eating, and, more important, stop drinking, and still be kept comfortable? She is reassured. It took only six days for a peaceful and good death.

The nurses who care for the dying in hospice programs know all about this way, and have known it for years. They also know how to manage all sorts of discomforts, and that when they use opiates they give enough by skillful ways that unfortunately are little known by most of us doctors. They have seen patients, who have had enough of a life that is surely ending, turn their faces to the wall and refuse all food and drink, and they know that with good nursing care and attention to anxiety and pain they need not suffer.

In a recent study in Washington State of physicians' attitudes toward assisted suicide 48% thought euthanasia was never justified, and 42% disagreed, but only 33% would be willing to perform euthanasia. A little over half thought assisted suicide should be legal in some instances, but only 40% would assist a patient commit suicide.[3]

Legal or not, physicians will occasionally assist in suicide; if we made it legal we could provide employment for a whole new crowd of lawyers and regulators. I am told that in the Netherlands, where it has become fashionable to euthanize, the records are not well kept, and many are dispatched without their consent. If it were legal here, that problem of less-than-voluntary euthanasia would be inevitable even though we may be more adept at regulating than the Dutch! In those, situations where physicians and families agree that death is the best solution but the patient has not yet been brought around to that point of view, fear of the law tends to stay their hand. It should be left that way.

Our assignment, it seems to me, is to reassure our dying patients that we will stay by them, that we will do all in our power to relieve their pain and spare them from inhumane and degrading treatment, that we will, in short, do our utmost to guide them, with the help of others, to a good death. We may often fail, but counseling suicide is just another of those ways to rid ourselves of burdensome lives. Surely we have seen enough of that in this century.

REFERENCES

1. Selzer R: *Letters to a Young Doctor*. New York: Simon and Schuster; 1982:70–4.
2. Eddy DM: A conversation with my mother. *Conn Med* 1994; 58:483–6. *JAMA* 1994; 272:179–81. Reprinted with permission.
3. Cohen JS, Fihn SD, Boyko EJ, et al: Attitudes toward assisted suicide and euthanasia among physicians in Washington State. *N Engl J Med* 1994; 331:89–94.

Connecticut Medicine 1994; 58(8):502

Last Things: Planning Ahead

IN my first year of practice an older clinical colleague—he was at least 40—gave me advice about caring for a terminally ill patient; he said that when the time came to decide whether to persist in treatment or to ease the patient's departure, I should not discuss it with the family. That would inflict a heavy burden which they would have to bear for the rest of their lives; we could shoulder things more easily, he said, and the obligation clearly belonged to physicians to do so.

All that was before the days of cardiopulmonary resuscitation, ventilators, pacemakers, even intensive care units, and the new morality. The most effective action we might take was to reduce the flow of oxygen into the tent, slow the intravenous drip, and increase the morphine. Hardly noticeable to anyone but the nurses and they rarely mentioned it; they knew what was happening, probably thought it overdue, not worthy of comment, and continued with their good nursing care. Several times I had seen this taking place when I was a resident, and had talked briefly about it with fellow house officers or attendings, a conversation which usually concluded with an expression of hope that someone would do the same for us one day.

Unfortunately we cannot count on that anymore. Hardly a week passes now in which someone does not have a painful tale to tell of the family too filled with sorrow to make such hard decisions, the hospital administrator who is worried about legal implications, and the patient whose wishes can no longer be expressed. Physicians know, they have been told often enough, these decisions are no longer theirs to make.

It may be just as well; some doctors may have misused their privileged position. I remember a professor of medicine who claimed to be responsible but not generally accountable; that was risky ground to occupy. But too much time spent accounting may mean that some hard decisions are never made or are made by default. The patient suffers for this higher morality and society pays.

That is why I was delighted to see a living will in a home-care patient's chart last month. Not just the simple statement about not being "kept alive through life support systems if my condition is deemed terminal," but she had written and initialed specific directions about what not to do: no tube feeding, no intravenous fluids, no antibiotics, no attempted resuscitation, no midnight trips to the hospital. Here there was no ambiguity; it was clear that she and her physician had worked this thing out with care. Her closest family members had signed as witnesses. The nurses who will look after her are prepared to reassure themselves from time to time that this remains an expression of her wishes.

Whenever I hear doctors, or the medical establishment, being criticized about inhuman technologies and exorbitant costs, this matter of the high cost of dying, or the cruel prolongation of life, almost always takes center stage. Young people blame us for it as though they had just discovered what we had failed to see; the elderly want to talk about it. Yet I have seen few living wills in medical records, and, when I have asked them, most older patients tell me that their doctors have never mentioned the matter. Is it a physician's professional duty to bring up the subject? There are some of us who are such efficient planners that, in the bloom of perfect health, we have drawn up our living wills, have had them witnessed, and have filed them where our families, physician, executor, and lawyer will easily find them. But more of us avoid thinking about such things, and, unless we feel the shadows closing in, would never without prompting take the step.

If we and our patients are to be spared torturing delays and ruinous indecision at the end, we must raise the issue of a living will or its equivalent before the difficult time comes. It will then be simpler to follow the advice given in the textbook I used over 40 years ago:

> Now irksome restrictions should be modified and distasteful therapy limited. Finally comes the stage when opium in some form alone will bring surcease to suffering; it should not be spared at this stage.[1]

REFERENCE

1. Christian HA: *The Principles and Practice of Medicine* (Osler) ed. 15. New York and London: D. Appleton Century; 1944:1066.

Connecticut Medicine 1987; 51(10):687

The Undiscovered Country

IN conversations with residents and geriatric fellows, the matter of end-of-life decision making, living wills, and durable power of attorney is certain to come up, as it should. Always they feel an uneasiness, not so much about death, but rather how to talk about it with patients. Understandable because most of these young physicians have never actually seen someone die, never witnessed the hours and minutes before death, never talked at length with patients, young or old, who know their disease is fatal and that they are dying. Many 30-year-olds, in fact, have four living grandparents, or if one has died, that death took place in Florida or Iowa, miles away. Death is like Timbuktu; they know it exists but they've never been there.

As a matter of fact, talking with the dying about death is something few of us have done; so how are we to talk with healthy patients about their desires at the end of life? As professionals, can we tell them much more than they already know about this experience that we all will one day face, how it is likely to happen, what will be done to them when they are helpless, and where? That most of us want this kind of information was dramatically demonstrated by the great popularity of Dr. Sherwin Nuland's best seller, *How We Die* [1994].

The first physician to attempt a study of this matter, using Pierre Louis's "Numerical System," was William Osler. He wrote of his study, done in the Johns Hopkins Hospital, recounting his findings in his Ingersoll lecture, *Science and Immortality*, in 1904:

> I have careful records of about five hundred death-beds, studied particularly with reference to the modes of death and sensations of the dying. The latter alone concerns us here. Ninety suffered bodily pain or distress of one sort or another, eleven showed apprehension, two positive terror, one expressed spiritual exaltation, one bitter remorse. The great majority gave no sign one way or the other; like their birth, their death was a sleep and a forgetting. The Preacher was right: in this matter man hath no pre-eminence over the beast,—as the one dieth so dieth the other.

Surprisingly only four or five other studies of this kind have been done since, the most recent being by Joan Lynn et al that appeared in *Annals of Internal Medicine* last month (15 January 1997; 126:97–106). This study involved 9,105 seriously ill patients in five teaching hospitals of whom 4,124 died. In the last three days, 55% were conscious, 40% had severe pain, and 63% "had difficulty tolerating physical or emotional symptoms." Twenty-five percent had a ventilator, 40% a feeding tube. Over half had indicated a desire for comfort care, and 10% were treated contrary to their preferences. The authors conclude with a carefully worded comment:

> It is likely that quality of care at the end of life will have to be routinely measured and that the public and other health care purchasers will have to demand and pay for adequate performance before lasting and sustained improvements are possible (p.105).

Arthur W. Feinberg in an editorial in this same issue suggests separate hospital units for dying patients (hospice units?), or "keep the dying patient out of the high-technology milieu of the hospital," and notes that "Our society has not yet accepted the inevitability of death."

I would suggest that we had a better time of it in 1904 than now; from my discussions with hospice nurses I know that pain and distress, physical, mental, and spiritual, can be controlled over 90% of the time by skillful, intelligent, and empathic care, even beating Osler's experience of 75% whose "death was a sleep and a forgetting," not the wild death in the ICU!

Dr. Bernard Lown in his recent book *The Lost Art of Healing* (Houghton Mifflin, New York, 1996) wastes no words:

> Reflecting on a life of dealing with death and dying, I am persuaded that death's anguish is, in no small measure, man made. It is a product of Western culture, which denies death its due and foolishly allocates mammoth resources to prolong the tormenting act of dying. . . . But it is difficult to see any change. . . . the economics of dying are too great, and doctors too deeply fixated on proving their power over death, for the system to yield. . . .
>
> Any meliorization of the problem has to face up to the fact that the contempory hospital functions best when the patients are infantilized and disempowered. . . . hospitals [must be] decoupled from the act of dying (pp. 288–9).

Rather than demanding that we fix this "unintended effect" of our good intentions, half of our patients are now asking us to become their willing executioners to save them from a demeaning fate far worse than death! What a shame!

Connecticut Medicine 1997; 61(2):121

Tragic Fall or Angle of Repose?

A rift in the clouds in a gray day threw a shaft of sunlight upon her coffin as her nervous, energetic little body sank to its last sleep. But the soul of her, the glowing, gorgeous, fervent soul of her, surely was flaming in eager joy upon some other dawn.

William Allen White (1868–1944)

WILLIAM Allen White was editor of the *Emporia Gazette*, a most admirable newspaper back in the early decades of this century. He wrote a tribute to his daughter, Mary White, a high-school student whose funeral had been just the day before, and the quotation above was its final paragraph. Mary, an excellent rider, had been knocked off her horse by a low-hanging limb as she looked back to wave to a friend. She had just been accepted to enter Wellesley the next year, 1922.

We read White's essay in high-school American Lit back in 1937. I have read it several times since. We read many essays, poems, short stories and novels in that class and in English Literature the next semester. Most of them have remained more or less in memory, and, I believe, have made a difference. A surprising number had to do with death—but not the violent, gory, obscene, and diabolical deaths with their criminal or sexual overtones that we permit our entertainers to spew upon our children in these enlightened *fin-de-siècle* years.

Deaths of young men and women, deaths of children, are deeply tragic. Samuel Johnson called every death violent "which is not gradually brought on by the miseries of age, or when life is extinguished for any other reason than that it is burned out. He that dies before 60, of a cold or consumption, dies, in reality, by a violent death."

During my public school years in the 1920s and '30s, I recall four deaths among my contemporaries: three died before the age of 10, two from meningitis, one an accident; the fourth, a 16-year-old classmate died suddenly from a cerebral hemorrhage. Five adult members of my family died in those same years, two aunts, my grandfather, and two great-grandparents. I believe this was in no way unusual. Today the first three deaths, ages 33, 51 and 64, could undoubtedly have been prevented. My great-grandparents were "burned out," both in their 10th decade, ready to go.

Last month, George Will, one of my favorite columnists, wrote of his father's death at age 89 [*Chicago Sunday Times*, April 4, 1998]. Even some of my more liberally-minded friends and relations, rarely given to mentioning George Will except in anger, admitted that it was a first-rate essay. He quoted a line, ". . . when the 'summons comes to join the innumerable caravan.'" American Lit came to mind and I recognized, from some 60-year-old storage place, William Cullen Bryant's *Thanatopsis:*

> So live, that when thy summons comes to join
> The innumerable caravan which moves
> To that mysterious realm, . . .

Will had written of his father's death that "He was, it is safe to say, not sorry when the Dark Angel tapped him on his shoulder and said it was time to go," [adding]:

> In earlier ages, much was made of the *ars moriendi,* the art of dying, of having "a good death." Nowadays, science often overwhelms that art. When death approaches the elderly on measured tread, they are apt to become tangled in the toils of modern medicine. Then the dying are pushed to the side of the stage as medicine becomes the leading actor. . . . medicine becomes problematic when it resists not the body's afflictions but the body itself.

In high-school English Literature among the many required memorizations were, of course. Hamlet's "To be, or not to be," and Browning's *Prospice*:

> Fear-death?—To feel the fog in my throat,
> The mist in my face
> When the snows begin, and the blasts denote
> I am nearing the place . . .

Another was Kipling's *E'nvoi*:

> When Earth's last picture is painted, and the tubes are twisted and dried,
> When the oldest colors have faded, and the youngest critic has died,
> We shall rest, and faith, we shall need it—lie down for an aeon or two,
> Till the Master of All Good Workmen shall set us to work anew!

How delightfully late Victorian that now seems. But when I first read his poem, Kipling had been dead only one year! My father's favorite lines, which we also had to memorize, were from Tennyson's *Crossing the Bar*, always placed at the end of any edition of the Laureate's poetry:

Sunset and evening star,
  And one clear call for me!
And may there be no moaning of the bar,
  When I put out to sea,

But such a tide as moving seems asleep,
  Too full for sound and foam,
When that which drew from out the boundless deep
  Turns again home.

Twilight and evening bell,
  And after that the dark!
And may there be no sadness of farewell,
  When I embark;

For though from out our bourne of Time and Place
  The flood may bear me far,
I hope to see my Pilot face to face
  When I have crossed the bar.

Will tells us that his father's favorite modern novel was Wallace Stegner's *Angle of Repose.* It is one of mine also. Angle of repose is a mining engineering term for "the angle at which sliding dirt and debris come to rest." It is a perfect metaphor, as Stegner and Will both point out, for the point in our decline at which we come finally and mercifully to rest, our angle of repose. Of his father he wrote, "Fred left life as he lived it, nobly composed, having reached his angle of repose."

My antique generation learned from poetry and narrative, which is the best way, to come to accept death as part of living, although we never used that kind of psychobabble. We never considered death to be unusual or an option, or that heroics were called for to stave it off when the jig was up. Cemeteries were all over the place, and we visited the graves of our dead friends and relatives from time to time on sunny Sunday afternoons, and almost always on Memorial Day, just to say hello and that we still remembered, and, perhaps unspoken, perhaps not, "We'll be seeing you one of these days!"

Our medical schools have recently rediscovered death, and, like the rest of us, have begun to listen to the complaints from those who depend upon us that physicians, or most of us, don't know beans about death and dying, that too often we walk away, or do things to and for our patients that are quite inappropriate. Sherwin Nuland says that we have allowed ourselves to become "besotted" with our science and technology. That may be. We do have a moral obligation to understand and know how to apply this amazing science and technology; we also have an obligation to know when to withhold it. William Osler knew that, in part because he had little science and technology to withhold. He wrote of the dying he had observed: “The great majority gave no signs one way or another; like birth, their death was a sleeping and a forgetting.”

Connecticut Medicine 1998; 62(4):245–6

Section 6—Technology

It has become appallingly obvious that our technology has exceeded our humanity.

Albert Einstein (1879–1955)

The vitality of thought is in adventure. Ideas won't keep. Something must be done about them.

Alfred North Whitehead (1861–1947)

"Things Are in the Saddle"

MAN'S technology, what it does and how much it costs, has dominated the talk of economists, political scientists, philosophers, poets, engineers, and scientists for a century at least. Most of us who grew up with 20th-century technology probably did not think much about it, except to be proud that Americans invented so many useful things. After World War II, we worried about the Bomb and then about television and its effects on our children's minds; suddenly a whole mass of problems about highways, pollution, nuclear energy, and the relations between technology and political power have been raised, and nobody seems ready with explanations or even very good questions.

While science and technology represent separate human endeavors and follow different rules, they are related in our heads; thought and act, mind and hand are too closely linked to go on separately for long. Our ability to find out more about nature and to build new machines seems almost limitless. Victor Weisskopf wrote that, " — potentially, science can justifiably claim the ability to understand every observable phenomenon."[1]

New knowledge opens the way to new technologies; these new tools are the means to new knowledge, and so almost *ad infinitum*, the "almost" having to do with how far we are willing to push our materialism.

Our science is at most a 10th as old as our civilization which, as far as we can tell, has been around for less than one percent of the time that we have had our present kind of central nervous systems. We have hardly begun, and it is difficult to imagine limits.

And yet there are doomsayers. Philip Handler, in a recent editorial in *Science*,[2] says that, "The intellectual elite in every era has always been pessimistic." There seems everywhere to be an increasing antiscience and antitechnology mood that may be more than recurring 19th-century romanticism. It has to do with fears not easily put to rest; Goethe was haunted by the Faust legend most of his life; this matter of the good and evil uses of knowledge lies at the heart of his drama. There are hard philosophical problems that are not passed over by saying that science and technology are morally neutral.

In medicine it should not be so difficult. Our technologies have been mostly beneficent and have been, in Francis Bacon's words, "for the benefit and use of life"(1623). Stethoscopes, clinical thermometers, poliomyelitis vaccine, and even CT scanners do not sully the neighborhood, dirty the water, or provide anyone with undue political power. On the surface, they raise no serious philosophical questions.

There are problems, nonetheless. Technologies which should be means have a way of becoming ends. Sometimes we forget to ask what the technology is for or why the answer is worth having. Howard Spiro writes, "Gastroenterologists and radiologists, trading plastic cards and pictures, sometimes look very much like the boys of my youth trading baseball cards."[3] We are worried about how this love affair with machines, images, and numbers may dull the edge of our clinical acumen, make us brokers between people and machines, create ugly bureaucracies, and drive up the cost of care.

This last is the least important; at most, it qualifies only as a symptom. Most technologies, properly used, are cheaper than those they replace; effective technologies like vaccines are cheapest and best of all.

If technology adds to cost without improving care, it does so in the little decisions made thousands of times every day—questions that are put to machines and laboratory technicians whose answers make no difference. The regulators do not know how to get at that, but they can limit the availability of the big and effective technologies that do make a difference but probably add little to costs.

Better education in the skillful and artistic use of existing technologies is half the answer; more research to get better explanations of biology and more powerful technologies, which are almost always cheaper, is the other half. Attacking the symptom of dollar costs head on may make everything worse by taking away initiative, increasing real costs, and dismantling a system of medical care that for all its faults is the best in the world.

REFERENCES

1. Weisskopf V: The frontiers and limits of science. *Bull Am Acad Arts Sci* 1975; 28:15–26.
2. Handler P: Public doubts about science. *Science* 1980; 208:1093.
3. Spiro HM: The physician and the ikon. *Pharos* 1980; 48:2–5.

Connecticut Medicine 1980; 44(7):459

Words Without End

IN an older agricultural society most work, or the intensity of work, was seasonal. The cycle of sowing, cultivating, and harvesting began and ended, and the winter which followed was a time of relative quiet. In the cities the seasons of work were turned around, in part because it was easier before air conditioning to heat the schools and factories in winter than to cool them in summer. Except for farmers, obstetricians, and sailors, the pace of living slowed down in the warm months, and society organized itself in such a way as to permit these recurring cycles of work and leisure. Even diseases were seasonal, and the intestinal complaints of summer made less demand on the hospitals than the respiratory illnesses of winter.

We would need to examine the records to see what happened in the hospitals during a 19th-century summer; I suspect that many of the long wards were bright, breezy, and nearly empty. In teaching hospitals, doctors, especially the chiefs, were on holiday or attending international congresses.

In his biography of William Osler, Cushing writes of long summer holidays with travel to Canada and abroad. In 1890, Osler left for Freiburg in May and returned to Baltimore from Berlin in September. Following his marriage in May 1892, he and Grace Revere Osler left for Canada, then crossed the Atlantic to Southampton, spent the summer in Devon and Cornwall, and returned home in August. Some summer holidays were shorter, some were longer, but they were all times of renewal; in 1903, he sailed on May 29th for England and returned from Paris on September 10th. Osler wrote of the need for quinquennial brain-dusting, and those were the longer summers, the *Studienreisen.*

The late 20th century has conspired against both leisure and privacy. There is little time to create because there is too much to do; no time to read because there is too much to read. It may be that we have fled into frenetic activity because we find leisure worthless and privacy lonely, but I suspect electronic technology has more to do with it. These devices have given us giant sense organs disproportionate to our brains.

Cheap and instantaneous communication has removed one of the brakes on nervous activity. There is so much information chasing around circuits into which we are all wired that we cannot stop responding. Only ordinary speech and the mail are slow by contrast.

Now that last safeguard is about to disappear. We are to have electronic mail! Everyone will have a word processor which will provide information at the rate of 10,000 characters per second. It is bad enough to think of "processing" words; imagine sending these electronic compositions instantaneously to anyone and everyone whenever the switch is on. Surely then the lid will be off.

All of this is supposed to save time, and should, in consequence, make room for more creative work, even allow leisure for brain-dusting. But that would only be so if these machines could be bridled, compelled to store or transmit no more than our present burden of information, disciplined into some sort of steady state. We do not have need even for this much, but of the making of words there is no end, and words and symbols will surely multiply to the full capacity of all the instruments, no matter if the characters per second increase a hundred fold, which by the law of technology they will.

The photocopier, the computer printer, the CRT [cathode ray tube], the video screen, and the telephone by now have us nearly swamped; the word processor will surely finish the job.

Our capacity to make sense of increasing masses of incoming data must follow a rising and falling curve in a manner analogous to Starling's law of the heart. By flooding us with words and thereby rendering leisure unthinkable, we must surely decompensate, and, since we shall all be linked by our word processors, we can take comfort in failing together like the cells in a myocardial syncytium. That, rather than a nuclear holocaust, may be the final epidemic—"not with a bang but a whimper."[1]

REFERENCE

1. Eliot TS: The Hollow Men, in *The Complete Poems and Plays*, 1909–1950. New York: Harcourt Brace and Company; 1950:56–9.

Connecticut Medicine 1982; 46(6):355

Cost of Care or Burden of Disease?

IF health is the goal of medicine, then prevention of disease or cure are the proper objectives. In Lewis Thomas's words, prevention and cure are accomplished by the *high technology* of medicine, and represent the task completed. This technology has the distinguishing marks of simplicity and economy, and springs from an understanding of the basic nature of the disease. The expensive technologies are what Dr. Thomas calls *half-way technologies*, and they are generally uncertain, expensive, impressive, and add little that is new to our understanding.

The rising cost of care has given us a new expression: *cost-containment,* and a set of dogmas about the cause and cure of what may be an inevitable economic development. Our regulators insist that the growth of *their* work is inevitable in our complicated society; the cost of government is rising more rapidly than that of health care.

One of the dogmas is that new technologies add significantly to the cost of medical care. "The growth of technology has shaped services to a larger degree than patients' needs or desires or prudent expenditure patterns would justify," according to David Mechanic.[1] This may be, but surely he is not thinking of poliomyelitis vaccine, antibiotics, defibrillators, or neonatal intensive care units as causing imprudent expenditures. Even the half-way technologies, once developed, become less expensive, and, used with judgment, reduce the burden of disease.

Certainly there are anecdotes about expensive procedures which, in retrospect, may have been thought to be unnecessary, but it is doubtful that many new technologies can be shown to have increased costs without increasing benefits proportionally. Initially, new procedures add to costs, especially if they are subsequently shown to be ineffective, but the knowledge gained leads finally to an effective solution.

We should consider the burden of disease and how to reduce it rather than the cost of care and how to contain it. Decisions about whether to support new technology may not require new ways of thinking, but rather using several of the old ways together. In attempting to assess the value of coronary artery surgery, we need to review the results of earlier technologies that have been used and discarded. We shall find what the history of medicine has so often shown, that almost any therapeutic technology may look for awhile as if it were working. We also have to pay attention to the natural course of the disease; modern medicine has been around long enough for that.

We should recall that cost-effectiveness, if it can be known, is only one basis for making decisions. Rational beings can make irrational decisions based upon prejudice, taste, or mood. Wars have begun in anger, and battles have been lost by depressed generals, But thoughtful decisions are usually made for ethical reasons, for economic reasons, for political reasons, or for rational and scientific reasons. As physicians we believe that our clinical decisions are based upon both science and ethics, because our art rests upon both the biological sciences and our commitment to relieve suffering.

In deciding about medical technology, these same ethical and scientific considerations should apply, but others, using the rules of the marketplace or forum, will insist upon economic or political justification, never considering that these arguments would not be acceptable if applied to themselves. When the planners and regulators enforce their regulations, and other planners and regulators begin to be frightened about their own throbbing headaches or oppressive chest pains, there will be a call to return to reason and virtue, a protest that human life has no price tag. There are laws governing the provision of care which work as inexorably as the laws of the market place; only in a society without human values as we understand them are those laws identical.

Technology is forcing change at a rate greater than ever before; undoubtedly that change must be managed. Assessing technology is not a matter for political decision making, and cannot be settled by vote on the board of a Health Systems Agency. Whether a technology is useful is a matter for scientific inquiry; whether it should be used is an ethical question. If it is effective and should be used, a way to make it affordable will be found.

Computed tomography (CT) illustrates the problems of managing technological change. Its costs are high, but should be balanced against the costs of the technology that it has replaced. There are ethical reasons for using CT in the place of dangerous or painful alternative procedures. It is becoming cheaper, as happens with useful technologies. It will find a place in medicine in spite of the planners, and when all is tallied, the cost added to care by CT may be only that generated by the regulators in their efforts to control it.

REFERENCE

1. Mechanic D: Approaches to controlling the costs of medical care: Short-range and long-range alternatives. *N Engl J Med* 1978; 298(5):249–54.

Connecticut Medicine 1978; 42(4):263

Fides Medici

IT was pleasant to find that my 1952 unabridged Webster's International Dictionary does not have the word *holism*, nor does the Oxford. It does appear in Webster's New Collegiate, 1971, and is derived from *hol-* plus *-ism*. That qualifies it as a barbarism: the first syllable is the English word *whole*, and the second is a Latin suffix, *-ism*. Dropping the *w* disguises the northern origin of *whole* and gives the word a Greek look. *Wholeness, integrity,* or *oneness* might have done, but perhaps there was need for a new word, and we should impoverish our language if we wiped out all words of hybrid derivation. Fowler's comments are about right:

> That barbarisms should exist is a pity; to expend much energy on denouncing those that do exist is a waste; to create them is a grave misdemeanor; and the greater the need of the word that is made, the greater its maker's guilt if he miscreates it.[1]

The phrase *holistic medicine* appears more and more often in the press and in lecture circuits to signify some sort of medicine different from the kind currently practiced. Those opposed to technology in hospitals, chemotherapy for cancer, lithium for depression, reductionism in biology, and research in medical schools speak of holistic medicine as an alternative to whatever it is that allopaths do. Not all would admit to motives of antiscience or antitechnology. Certainly we all know that in our zeal to cure we may lose sight of the patient as a person. In attending to the part we may forget the whole; instead of treating patients we may deal with clients in our ponderous bureaucracies, the hospitals and clinics.

But many of the holists seem to have broken with scientific medicine, or at least hide their hostility with difficulty. Another cult may be no more risky than Christian Science, chiropractic, or homeopathy, all of whose origins were intertwined with a thread that runs right on into holistic medicine. Tragedies occur when cultic principles are doggedly applied, but the greater danger is in letting the virus of cultism into scientific medicine.

Except for a score or two of careful observers or devoted practitioners during the past three millennia, medical history until recently has been one of unrelieved failure. Only in the past 100 years has medicine begun to fulfill its promises. Although many of the great victories lie in the future, those that have been won may be ascribed to technological inventions and the growth of biological science.

The practice of medicine is an art; it is not only technology or applied science. It is the artistic use of both in caring for human beings in matters relating to their health. Without the science and the technology, the artistry would be only as effective as unassisted nature in eliminating disease and repairing injury. That capacity is by no means trivial, but to holistic medicine or megavitamins may be ascribed what is justly due to nature.

Because nature has selected well, we may waver in our faith in the power of science, but there can be no going back. Science will go on as long as we are around; there will always be more to know, another question to get an answer to, and, with each new understanding, our capacity to apply our art "for the benefit and use of life," as Francis Bacon hoped, increases.

Withdrawing from the high ground of science would not be accepted for long. Our minds wouldn't allow it; any retreat could delay some victories in medicine for decades.

When Alfred Russell Wallace, the 19th-century naturalist, broke with Darwin on the issue of human evolution because, although he believed that natural selection accounted for the origin of all other species, he could not accept it for man, Darwin wrote: "I differ grievously from you, and am very sorry for it."[2] He recognized that once our hands had seized the plow of science, there was no looking back.

REFERENCES

1. Fowler HW: *A Dictionary of Modern English Usage*. Oxford University Press; 1944:42.
2. Eiseley L: *Darwin and the Mysterious Mr. X.* New York: EP Dutton; 1979:29.

Connecticut Medicine 1980; 44(2):115

Section 7—Language and Writing

For the studies, first they should begin with the chief and necessary rules of some good grammar.

John Milton (1608–1674)

I have grown fond of semicolons in recent years. The semicolon tells you that there is still some question about the preceding full sentence; something needs to be added; it reminds you sometimes of the Greek usage.

Lewis Thomas (1913–1993)

On Words, Style, Grammar, and Other Matters

ONE day last month I was stopped in my tracks by two headlines in the *Hartford Courant*. The first on the front page top left:

**Lobbyists
Giveth;
Legislators
Taketh**

Eye-catching and true but grammatically dead wrong. The headline writer's attempt to write Elizabethan or Jacobean English failed; he had not recalled from his reading of the King James Bible or Shakespeare that the -(e)th verb ending is third person singular. But why should I assume that he had ever read either?

On an inside page I read:

**Let He Who Is
Without Sin . . .**

He was, of course, quoting from John 8:7, "He that is without sin among you, let him first cast a stone at her," but misquoted it, even failing to recognize, actually to sense, that "he" in this instance should be "him," object of the verb "let." Minor errors become major when printed in 18- or 30-point bold type.

Hypersensitivity to words and syntax may not be genetic but it can be acquired after a few years of copy-editing and proof-reading. My secondary editorial career began 60 years ago when I was editor of our high school newspaper, a triweekly, and later at Oberlin, as page editor on the *Review*, a semiweekly. After an interruption of over 50 years, I resumed this earlier career by accepting the editorship of both the *Journal of the History of Medicine and Allied Sciences* and *Connecticut Medicine*, the former for only four years. As another medical journal editor once commented, "One feels like the circus horse in the barn; when the band starts to play your hooves begin to stomp." An editor reads with a pencil or a red pen in his mind, if not in his hand.

All writers commit some mortal, but mostly venial sins; either variety that shows up on the printed page is more embarrassing to the editor, or should be, than to the author. Everyone who writes needs an editor. My wife and daughter are painfully critical editors who sometimes humiliate me by laughing at something not intended to be funny. Bob Brunell scans all the page proofs along with me just before this journal goes to the printer.

Misquotations, reporting cooked data, and writing such things as "studies have shown" are mortal sins. Wrong references are almost impossible to track down, and many reviewers and most editors choose to leave the writer unredeemed, sunk in his sin. "Most studies have shown," if without references, is almost always a lie.

Politically incorrect lines here and there are venial and rarely bother me, although I have become sensitive to exclusive use of the male third-person pronoun, but equally offended by "his or her," or worse still "his/her." Leaving the subject in the singular, "a patient," and then referring to "they, their, or them," is an abomination. Example: "Everyone should have a choice of their physician." Another example appeared in the *Courant*: "Each mother, no matter her circumstances, takes an optimistic gamble on the future, whether they know it or not."

All editors have words that they rarely permit to see the light of day; mine include: most vulgarity, "impact" used to mean affect or effect or consequence, "lifestyle," "reach out or outreach," "which" instead of "that" in a defining clause, and "in the context of." Joseph Epstein, former editor of *The American Scholar*, added a few more expressions of the "reach out" psychobabble-type: ". . . *special, caring, and sharing*," and I would add *healing* when the reference is not to wounds, ulcers, and fractures. Incidentally, his views of the words "gay" and "Lesbian" are the same as mine. A Lesbian is a native of the Greek isle of Lesbos, and gay, a perfectly fine word of ancient vintage (Chaucer used it) has been forever lost.

The world is full of books telling us how to write acceptable English. Among the classics are *A Dictionary of Modern English Usage*, by H.W. Fowler, usually referred to just as "The Fowler," and, by the same author, *The King's English*. The title dates it: first edition 1906, third edition 1931. These books are more fun to read than to use; for example:

SHALL AND WILL

> It is unfortunate that the idiomatic use, while it comes by nature to Southern Englishmen (who will find most of this section superfluous), is so complicated that those who are not to the manner born can hardly acquire it; and for them the section is in danger of being useless. In apology for the length of these remarks it must be said that the short and simple directions often given are worse than useless. The observant reader soon loses faith. . . . (*The King's English*, p. 142.)

For me *The Chicago Manual of Style* is quite adequate, and for the journal, *The American Medical Association Manual of Style (8th ed)* has served well for almost a decade. Anyone intending to write a medical article needs a copy close at hand. I have kept a "Strunk" by my typewriter, now word processor, for 35 years. *The Elements of Style* by William Strunk, Jr., was first published in 1937. Macmillan brought out a new edition in 1959 that had been somewhat revised and expanded by E.B.White (remember *Charlotte's Web*?). A professor of religion and Old Testament Hebrew asserted that E.B.White was the finest writer of English prose in the 20th century! If, by chance, you are unfamiliar with this gem, find a copy. Some examples of his straightforward style:

And/or—A device borrowed from legal writing. It destroys the flow and goodness of a sentence.

Can—Means *am* (*is, are*) able. Not to be used as a substitute for *may*.

Comprise—Literally *embrace*. A zoo *comprises* mammals, reptiles, and birds, (because it embraces, or includes, them). But animals do not *comprise* (embrace) a zoo— they *constitute* a zoo.

Contact—As a transitive verb, the word is vague and self important. Do not *contact* anybody; get in touch with him, or look him up, or phone him, or find him, or meet him.

Different than—Here logic supports established usage: one thing differs *from* another, hence *different from*. Or, *other than, unlike*.

In the eighth grade I took a course called General Language in which we learned about the history of the alphabet, the history of English, including a little Anglo-Saxon, more than a smattering of French, German, and Spanish, and a second semester devoted to Latin and enough Greek to recognize ΑΒΓΔ. I recall a formal debate by six students chosen by the teacher on the topic: Can we think without words? We were then asked to write a paper, taking one side or the other; I argued that without words thinking is impossible. Now I would argue that we cannot think in the way that human beings think without language. In his prologue, the author of St. John's gospel announced this with conviction, "In the beginning was the Word." He used, of course, the Greek *logos*, which my lexicon defines as "the word by which the inward thought is expressed, or reason itself."

I suppose that since the Hundred Years War, when Anglo-Saxon and Norman French slowly fused into something recognizable as English, Chaucer's English, the aging crowd has warned that the language of those under 30 was degenerate and incomprehensible. I recall reading some lines from the 15th-century printer, William Caxton, that appeared in the prologue to his translation of the *Eneydos* (Aeneid). He was apparently copy-editing his own prose:

> . . . I saw the fayr and straunge termes therein. . . . I doubted that it sholde not please some gentylmen whiche late blamed me, sayeng that in my translacyons I had over curyous termes whiche coude not be understande of comyn peple, & desired me to use olde and homely termes in my translacyons.

But it seems to me that something else is happening today; the language is becoming more and more imprecise. Science writing has not much suffered from this imprecision virus; in the physical and biological sciences the writers are up against verifiable reality. But in the social, psychological, and political sciences, as well as in the bureaucracies that are akin to these "sciences," such as education and management, and in the spreading crop of "studies," women studies, black studies, gender studies, obfuscation is the rule. Words or expressions such as *relate to, multiculturalism, diversity, validate, authenticate, value-laden, value-free, phallocentric, meaningful, significant other, disadvantaged, mentally challenged,* obscure rather than express thought, hardly the function of the *logos*. Rarely has this entered the medical literature except perhaps in the behavioral sciences and medical history or sociology. I quote an example:

> The narrative of the work is largely spatial grafting and making, moving and retaining. Given the histological basis of their analysis, this is what they see. But they also use the verbs of gift and display in the story of the rabbits. . . . What does the language habit tell us about the philosophy of these scientists? Are they really confused about the ontological status of their research animals, or the reality of what they are recording?[1]

If someone were to ask me to put this in my own words, I would be lost. Surely there is danger in encouraging too much of this sort of confusion in our language. Orwell's *1984* demonstrated that critical thinking can be effectively destroyed by making changes in the language that deprive it of meaning. Perhaps we need an Academy of the English Language, analogous to the Académie Français, with postmodernists and deconstructionists either excluded or in a tiny minority.

REFERENCE

1. Long DE: Moving reprints: A historian looks at sex research publications of the 1930s. *J Hist Med Allied Sci* 1990; 45:452–68, p.462.

Connecticut Medicine 1998; 62(5):305–6

"De Gustibus—"

"'WHEN I use a word,' Humpty-Dumpty said . . . , 'it means just what I choose it to mean—neither more nor less.'"[1]

In the old days, almost before living memory, the typist had to cut a stencil when a department head, dean, or some other university functionary needed more than four copies of a memorandum or letter. Care was taken not to run to more than one page. The Dictaphone with its waxed cylinders, the mechanical Underwood typewriter, and the school's one Mimeograph machine all conspired to enforce the virtue of brevity.

Now tape-recorders, word-processors, and the Xerox machine have reduced the time and effort needed to move a thought, rarely completely formed, from somewhere in the cerebral cortex to 150 single-spaced five-page copies. When all of the more backward departments have their word-processors, those copies can be distributed with the speed of light. All need for economy of words will be gone, and their numbers will rise like hospital costs in a world of third-party payers.

Technology is not the only culprit to be blamed for this glut of printed words: the new words themselves, stemming often from the same technology, are imprecise—or at least seem to be so—and three or four sentences may be needed to express the same notion which could have been compressed into one before the days of computer and bureaucratic jargon.

Those of us who are called upon to review memos and letters before they are distributed are often moved against charity to delete adjectives, rescue split infinitives, replace jargon with common English, and even eliminate entire sentences and paragraphs; we must resist, however, for if we admit to incomprehension of even one-quarter of the writer's nouns, how can we know precisely what he meant? Best leave it alone and worry only about typographical errors.

But if the letter requires our signature, or if the instructions are that the memorandum go forth "from your office," then I deem we may consider ourselves to be released. The blue pencil (now a felt-tipped pen) comes out, a comma is inserted before *and* between the last two members of a series, curving arrows lift out the adverbs which have been dropped into all the infinitives, and finally, without a second thought, a *delta* with a tail goes through two-out-of-every-three adjectives. The work has only begun, but already the bulk has been reduced by a third. Adverbs like *very, highly, importantly, essentially, significantly,* and *meaningfully* go along with the adjectives without our even considering the two-out-of-three rule.

Up until now the work has been fast and easy. The next step requires judgment. Who is to say that my taste in these matters is better than the writer's? For some, bottom line is a colorful expression; for others it is an overworked phrase often carrying the wrong idea. Some words may be killed outright, executed without mercy; like the executioner, KoKo, in the *Mikado*, "I've got a little list—I've got a little list."[2] I would begin with *thrust, focus, healthcare*, and *feedback*, and then go onto *input, arena, implement, task force, workshop, and/or, he/she, communicate, activate, ongoing, wholistic*, and *research* as a verb.

By now the writer's intent seems to emerge, and you find that his ideas may be reduced to two paragraphs, each with three simple sentences without a trace of the passive voice. But is that what the writer had in mind? These tasteless words do convey something, although it may not be the writer's meaning; a *dialogue* seems to some to be different from a *discussion*, and *thrust* means something different from *purpose*, but has the writer that distinction in mind? Very well then, if you are not to sign, undo your work, delete the deletions; but if your signature is required, "I conceive you may use any language you choose."[3] Otherwise we must forever hold our peace, seeking no upcoming, ongoing meaningful dialogue; we shall expect no feedback, and the thrust of the work to be meaningfully done will focus upon no significant arena. That is the bottom line, providing we can get it all onto one page. If we cannot redeem, at least we might confine the disorder: one page per functionary per month.

REFERENCES

1. Dodgson CL [Lewis Carroll]: *Alice's Adventures in Wonderland*, Chapter 6.
2. Gilbert WS: *The Mikado*, Act I.
3. Gilbert WS: *Iolanthe,* Act II.

Connecticut Medicine 1983; 47(1):51

IRV, sGaw, Raw, and Other Matters

THOSE of my friends who are real historians and can read medieval Latin texts excite in me the mortal sin of envy. With a dictionary in hand and some recall of four years of high-school Latin, I believe I could make it if only the monkish scribes in those dark and drafty scriptoria had not used so many abbreviations and such odd symbols. For example, St. John's Gospel in the Gutenberg 42-line Bible, certainly a copy of a manuscript, begins:

> In principio erat verbü: & verbü erat apud deû: et de9 erat verbü. O m̃ia p ip̃m facta sunt: & sine ip̃o factum est nichil.

Not bad, but, believe me, it gets worse; the inflected endings fade off into nothing, and all sorts of peculiar little symbols appear, like the 9 in the word that is clearly "deus." Couple that with Gothic letters that hardly match Jensen's Venetian type for clarity, and comprehension is remarkably impaired.

Something like this obscurity generally developed to set apart the powerful, learned, and priestly classes of society. The ancient Egyptians had two forms of writing: hieroglyphics, which means temple writing, and a cursive demotic form for ordinary people. In the early centuries of the present era Greek was the language of the upper classes in the Western Empire, and Latin was the vulgar tongue. Yet Latin became the language of scholarship in Western Europe until the early years of the last century. William Harvey used it in his lectures, except when the ancient tongue couldn't stand the strain, and he reverted to English, as in his 1616 Lumleian lecture where he inserts "as by two clacks of a water bellows to raise water" in his Latin text describing the passage of blood through the lungs and heart to the aorta.

In my medical school days we still used those beautiful symbols for ounces, drams, scruples, and grains, and lower-case Roman numerals for amounts, all centuries old. And we proudly learned the meaning of such esoteric combinations of letters as t.i.d., q.i.d., a.c., p.c., and h.s. Sometimes there was a barbaric mix of Latin and English, as in "Seconal gr iss at hs prn DNW." The delicious thing was that only the initiated knew what all that meant. There was even an HHH enema (high, hot, and a hell of a lot) for desperate situations.

Medical editors receive manuscripts replete with this kind of thing, but now in 1990s style. There is a list of abbreviations in the AMA Manual of Style, accompanied by the admonition always to spell out at first use. That list is obsolete a year after publication. Dictionaries of medical abbreviations are published; not more than 60% of acronyms appearing in submitted manuscripts ever make it into these. I recall laboratory tests of 50 years ago: CF & TT, VDB, II, WSS, GA & BD. Unexpanded these intruders would render papers from that time incomprehensible today.

In "Letters to the Editor" in this journal, a gastroenterologist complains of the exuberant growth of acronyms and other jargon, and has sent me a copy of a letter from a consultant, written, however, by a nurse practitioner, that shows how far this plague has spread. I think I betray no confidences by reproducing five lines of her letter:

> The patient was sent from the echo lab to the cath lab. Coronary angiography revealed (LM-10% distal, LAD-proximal 80%, Cx-70% before OM1, RCA-proximal 70%, normal LV). Surgical intervention was recommended.
>
> CABG was done on (date) (CABG x 6, Ao-PDA-LVbr, Ao-OM1-OM@, Ao-Diag, LIMA-LAD). . . .

As I read this I cannot shake the impression that the writer did not have a human being in mind at all, only a procedure, and even that not in three-dimensional clarity, but rather a piece of a procedure with neither past nor future. Apart from being incomprehensible to most physicians other than cardiac surgeons, it seems to me that language of this sort, if indeed it is language, diminishes the writer's view of the world, and is, in fact, dehumanizing. This letter as part of a medical record has no staying power; 10 years from now it might as well have been written in runic characters.

No doubt Standard English does not work for mathematics, nor for describing elementary particles like quarks and mesons. Immunologists may pull off such clusters as CD10(nT,nB;gpl00)J5 because they have to; no other way to do it. Try spelling that out at first use! But for most clinical reports, Standard English is the best thing going and its use forces the writer and reader both to comprehend and communicate. Besides obscuring, arcane language says clearly, "Hey, we're smarter than you guys." Worse than that, its habitual use dehumanizes in a profession that ought to be the most humane of the sciences.

Connecticut Medicine 1995; 59(10):631

In Praise of Being Amateur

"OBVIOUSLY the amateur will only indulge in so seemingly desiccated a pursuit if he enjoys it, and in the end no further justification need really be demanded."[1(374)] Sir Geoffrey Keynes was writing of his passion for bibliography, only one of his several pursuits, but what he had to say about playfulness in scholarship implied a gentle censure of some of the darker aspects of professionalism.

I first learned about Geoffrey Keynes, MD, FRCS, over 50 years ago; he had edited and written the introduction to an edition of Sir Thomas Browne's *Religio Medici* which my father had in his library, and which I was reading, along with a number of other books about doctors, during an early romantic encounter with medicine.

Years later I read his excellent biography of William Harvey in preparation for a talk on the author of *De Motu Cordis*, and discovered in addition his *Portraiture of William Harvey* from which I made some slides. At some time in the past 10 years I came to realize that Sir Geoffrey Keynes was the younger brother of John Maynard Keynes of Keynesian economics fame. His final book, *The Gates of Memory*, was published in 1981, only a year before his death at the age of 95. This delightful autobiography which reaches back from our decade into Victorian times celebrates a surgeon's life, but more especially the joys of amateur status, for Keynes was bibliographer, biographer, medical historian, art collector, wood worker, and *litterateur*. Nonetheless, until the end of his seventh decade he was first of all a surgeon: "Though my friends had often thought that literature and bibliography were my first loves, in reality it had been the other way round. My most intense interest had been in the science and practice of surgery. . . ."[1(307)]

His contributions to surgery were not inconsiderable. Following World War II, during which he had served in the R.A.F. [Royal Air Force], first as Group Captain, later as Acting Air Vice-Marshall, he returned to his old hospital, St. Bartholomew's, as Senior Surgeon; he was a "man of Bart's" as William Harvey had been over 300 years before.

During the First World War, as medical officer in the R.A.M.C. [Royal Army Medical Corps], he had pushed for the use of blood transfusions to reduce mortality from wounds, and had developed a drip-feed apparatus for controlling the rate of flow. The original work on the use of citrated blood had been an American development; Keynes learned it from a Harvard Medical School group in France in 1917. Shortly after the war his interest turned to the problem of breast cancer, and in 1922 he began to use radium needles, initially for those patients who were deemed inoperable. He later abandoned entirely the radical Halsted approach: "From 1929 onward I was publicly advocating conservative treatment for carcinoma of the breast."[1(216)] This involved him in many bitter controversies with his surgical colleagues, yet the 1982 edition of Garrison and Morton's *A Medical Bibliography*, lists his 1932 *British Journal of Surgery* article, "The radium treatment of carcinoma of the breast," among those texts which best illustrate the history of medicine.

While in the R.A.F. in 1942, he performed the first thymectomy in Great Britain for myasthenia gravis, following the lead of Alfred Blalock at Johns Hopkins in 1939. "By 1954 he had amassed the largest series of thymectomies in the world."[2] At the recommendation of the Royal College of Surgeons the Queen honored him with knighthood in 1955.

Nevertheless Keynes remains far better known to us for his amateur pursuits than for his work as a surgeon. Although more than once criticized by professional bibliographers for his "impure" scholarship and his rejection of some of the rules, he remained undaunted. "I preferred to give readers less pedantry and more humanity . . ." and he added, "In the ensuing years my 'impure' productions have continued to be in demand."

Increasingly the work of scholarship demands the skill and dedication of professionals, but unfortunately for the rest of us, professional scholars talk and write largely for one another whom they often regard more as competitors than as colleagues; worse yet they become deadly serious and possessive about the diminishing area of intellectual activity which they have staked out for themselves. The amateur on the other hand is there for the fun of it; his scholarship, though serious, retains a playful quality which invites us to return again and again to the joy of learning, "and in the end no further justification need really be demanded."

REFERENCES

1. Keynes G: *The Gates of Memory*. Oxford University Press; 1983.
2. Eaton LM, Clagett OT: Present status of thymectomy in the treatment of myasthenia gravis. *Am J Med* 1955; 19:703–17.

Connecticut Medicine 1987; 51(2):131

Section 8—The History of Medicine

History is the witness that testifies to the passing of time; it illumines reality, vitalizes memory, provides guidance in daily life and brings us tidings of antiquity.

Cicero (106-43 B.C.)

Whereof what's past is prologue.

William Shakespeare (1564–1616)

The History Seminar

THREE of us who were responsible for teaching the student elective seminar in the history of American medicine recently finished reading the student papers and then conducted our own *postmortem* on the course. As had been true in the past, the papers ranged from good to excellent; each student had done a small piece of historical research using both primary and secondary sources, and we all learned from their presentations in class, the faculty most of all because we got to read their papers.

Our educational objectives in this seminar are modest enough; we know that it is a refreshing interlude for students who are working their way through the difficult first year of the basic sciences; we hope they enjoy it, as the humanities should be enjoyed, and that those who have an interest in history derive some intellectual satisfaction from the work. We would like them to acquire some feeling for how medicine got here in the first place; how medicine, the science of human biology, and modern technology got together in the last 100 years to create the enterprise to which they have determined to devote their lives; how the history of medicine and science are essential for understanding the present as well as the past, and for providing some reasonable guesses about the future. For a few, the seminar may be the beginning of a life-long interest in the history of medicine.

Knowing that this may be our only chance, we do what teachers are most often tempted to do: we tend to talk too much, we attempt to tell too much, and, taking pains to leave nothing out, we skim superficially over more dates, names, and discoveries than anyone could possibly remember or have use for.

Not surprisingly, the students said that they would appreciate more reading assignments. Someone once observed that the need for the lecture was remarkably diminished when Gutenberg began printing in Mainz with moveable type; we seem to have forgotten that, but everytime that reform in medical education is in the air, the lecture comes under attack and a few hours are trimmed away. So it should be with history.

What history should be covered? The temptation is to begin with primitive medicine, start naming dates and names beginning with Imhotep [in ancient Egypt], and finish with a lecture on DeVries's implantation of the artificial heart or with a review of our notion of the risks of turning our hospitals and clinics over to investor-owned profit-making corporations. Rather than offering a seminar on the history of medicine, we should advise our students to read Paul Starr's *The Social Transformation of American Medicine (1982).*

What is needed is the background of a simpler time to show the interrelationships of religion, values, politics, law, economics, technology, and epidemiology with the science and the art of medical practice. That probably may be managed best with the Greek city-states of the fifth century B.C.; another choice might be 17th-century Europe. Everything else may then be skipped until we get to the last 100 years or so. In Connecticut we might begin a little earlier, taking in William Beaumont [surgeon, experimental physiologist, 1785–1853] and Horace Wells [dentist, pioneer in the use of anesthesia, 1815–1848].

The aim is to help the students to see the present and maybe a little of the future from the standpoint of history, to think of scientific and social events in an historical way; to feel in their bones that medicine and the human enterprise are inseparably bound together; and that the way we affect the future depends ultimately upon what we value.

Connecticut Medicine 1985; 49(7):481

Twilight of the Heroes?

"THE Heroic Physician in Literature: Can the Tradition Continue?" was the title of an address given by Anne Hudson Jones at the American Osler Society Meeting almost six years ago. The heroes she spoke of were doctors in literary works, the very ones that affected many of us during our more plastic premedical-school days: Tertius Lydgate in George Eliot's *Middlemarch*, Max Gottlieb in Sinclair Lewis's *Arrowsmith*, and several others. In passing she recalled A.J. Cronin's *The Citadel*. The hero physician in this 1937 novel was Andrew Manson. After I had finished reading about this heroic young Scots physician, I recall wishing that someday I might be Manson, bringing modern medicine to some remote place. During that same summer I read Vallery-Radot's *The Life of Pasteur* and Eve Curie's *Madame Curie*. My personal pantheon was taking shape.

Encounters with Lydgate and Gottlieb were to come later. I came to know more about Sinclair Lewis, his association with the University of Michigan, and how *Arrowsmith's* Max Gottlieb was drawn from the character of Frederick George Novy, the bacteriologist at Ann Arbor in the early decades of this century. It happened that my father's cardiologist was Novy's son, and I believe the two of them spent more time talking about Sinclair Lewis and Dr. Arrowsmith than about my father's ventricular septal defect.

Professor Jones analyses the attributes of the heroic physician in literature, "great talent, a keen intellect employed in the rigorous search for truth, and a savage disregard for material rewards and earthly honors," and "one more—compassion. . . ."

But heroes to work their magic should be drawn from real life—they may be long dead, but they must at one time have drawn breath from the very air that we breath, have walked on soil and labored in places very like our own, and faced all the trials and limits of our human condition. For many in my generation, and Dr. Arrowsmith's, William Osler was one, perhaps the greatest, of them all. He was spoken of frequently in medical school, we used his textbook—mine was the 15th edition, edited by Henry Christian. It still carried the dedication to William Arthur Johnson, priest of the parish of Weston, Ontario, James Bovell of the Toronto School of Medicine, and Robert Palmer Howard, Dean and Professor at McGill. My wife gave me a copy of Harvey Cushing's *The Life of Sir William Osler* during my third year in medical school. We once drove into Ontario looking for his birthplace at Bond Head near Dundas—it was only about 150 miles from Detroit—but no one we asked had ever heard of him. But of course, heroes are heroic only to a few.

The word "hero" sounds Greek, and indeed it is: *heros*, a warrior and others of the Trojan age, including even leeches and minstrels, superior to anyone living since, including demigods, according to my lexicon those offspring of one divine parent such as Asklepios, Achilles, Hercules. Professor Jones places the heroic age in medicine, or at least as represented in literature, as roughly between 1850 and 1950. Since mid-century the notion of heroism in medicine has been in danger, if not in decline. She names four likely reasons:

> [F]irst the remarkable success of medical technology in keeping bodies alive indefinitely (with the concomitant high costs); second the continuing impotence of medicine to cure many diseases—represented most powerfully by AIDS; third, the social changes in gender roles; and, fourth, the assault on Western values by an increasingly multicultural population.

I would add a fifth: how could a member of the *health-care industry*, or a *health provider*, a mere technician ever be heroic? "Ironically," Jones observed, "in a time when medical miracles are commonplace, physicians in literature are oddly unheroic. The heroic tradition has been displaced by satire, more bitter now than it was in the earlier comic tradition."

Thomas Carlyle, in his *On Heroes, Hero-Worship, and the Heroic in History*, written over 150 years ago, did not include physicians, only gods, prophets, poets, priests, men of letters, and kings. William Osler, 54 years younger than Carlyle, had five portraits over his mantel, both in Baltimore and at Oxford: his three medical heroes, Linacre, Sydenham, and Harvey, as well as the Baltimore physician Horatio C. Wood, who was influential in his Hopkins appointment, and John Henry, Cardinal Newman. Speak of Linacre, Sydenham, Harvey, even Osler or Halsted, to almost any three medical students or residents today and their looks would be uncomprehending. I've tried it.

Connecticut Medicine 1998; 62(11):687

Getting to the Heart of the Matter

> Igitur corde percusso sanguis multus fertur, venae elanguescunt, . . . matura mors sequitur.
>
> *Celsus, V, 26. 8.*

"NOW when the heart is penetrated, much blood issues, the pulse fades away, . . . death quickly follows." A Roman *medicus*, Aulus Cornelius Celsus, made this hardly original observation early in the first century. Aristotle had said the same thing over three centuries earlier, and before that Hippocrates is said to have written that "Penetrating wounds of the bladder, brain, heart, diaphragm, intestines, stomach or liver, are fatal." Until a century ago it was believed that even touching the myocardium would result in death. The great Theodor Billroth (1829–1894) had written "The surgeon who ever attempts to stitch up a wound in the heart may be certain that he will lose all his colleagues' respect forever."

Just 100 years ago this fall, Ludwig Rehn, a surgeon at Frankfurt am Main, closed a knife wound in the right ventricle of Wilhelm Justus, who had been stabbed following a tavern brawl, and the victim recovered. A similar feat had been attempted at least twice before, once in September 1895 by a Norwegian surgeon, Cappelen, and again in June 1896 by an Italian surgeon, Guido Farina, but in each case the patient survived less than five days. Rehn's patient was still alive and well 10 years later. There had been rabbit experiments with cardiac wound closure in the 1880s and some dog experiments in 1895, but as far as I know, there had been no successful cardiac surgery on a human being before that dramatic September night in Frankfurt in 1896.

In 1942, my first year in medical school, I had the good fortune to watch the surgical closure of a patent ductus at the University Hospital in Ann Arbor, thanks to a fourth-year medical student and good friend who was on his surgical rotation and managed to get me into the OR. As a medical intern during my required surgical rotation I scrubbed with Conrad Lam and held a retractor while he performed the first Taussig-Blalock procedure in Michigan on a young girl with tetralogy of Fallot.

A year or so later I can recall exactly where I was when I heard the incredible news from a fellow resident about Dwight Harken's and Charles Bailey's successful *intracardiac* operations for mitral stenosis.

More than a decade after that, in 1959 in Atlantic City, Mason Sones presented his paper and showed slides or a movie of coronary artery catheterization and angiography at the Cleveland Clinic. Afterward he and I met for a beer and to talk about his amazing pictures and gossip about our years as residents together at the Henry Ford Hospital. That bar is as vivid in my mind as a color photograph, and so is a cocktail party in Albuquerque in December 1967 where a close friend and cardiologist asked me if I'd heard the news that a South African surgeon, Christiaan Barnard, had successfully transplanted the heart of a 24-year-old woman to a 53-year-old man. I hadn't, and I found it unbelievable. I had always thought that, the heart being such a wonderfully simple pump, as William Harvey had noted, a mechanical heart should be a relatively simple device—much easier to design than an artificial kidney.

My father had congenital heart disease, a left-to-right shunt which was thought to be a patent ductus, but which proved at autopsy to be a large interventricular septal defect. He died at age 52; that was in 1948, and although he had been cyanotic for years, he was minimally troubled by his badly designed heart until the last few years when he began to have recurrent pulmonary emboli. He was an engineer by education and never could understand, knowing the pressure differences, why a patent ductus should result in cyanosis; I recall him telling me that he must have a frog's heart, three chambers, and that accounted for his cyanosis. He was right. It had been my dream before he died that some bright engineer would come up with a workable mechanical heart; I never thought seriously of transplantation.

In his 1956 book. *The Century of the Surgeon*, Jürgen Thorwald recounts, with some justifiable literary license, the story of Ludwig Rehn's dramatic suturing of Wilhelm Justus's stabbed right ventricle just 100 years ago. The tale is in the book's last chapter, "The Inner Sanctum," and Thorwald concludes with these words:

> Rehn had opened up for the surgeon a part of the human body which had hitherto been considered an inviolate sanctum. The door was open, and henceforth there would be no stopping the surgeon's scalpel.

"The heart," da Vinci wrote, ". . . moves of itself and does not stop unless forever." Leonardo, you were wrong!

Connecticut Medicine 1996; 60(11):693

Curiosity: An Aperitif

BEFORE beginning a lecture or seminar in the history of medicine, I feel an unpleasantness rising in the back of my neck; I have an inkling that most of the students are wondering why we waste their time in this way. So I stumble around with the question that my imagination has put into their heads: why bother about history? We have a CD-ROM in the library with the last five years of medical literature compressed onto it. Who needs more?

My answers, offered before they think to ask, vary, but generally include:

1. Curiosity, the same reason most of us would like to see Leningrad or poke around on the Martian desert.
2. To know ourselves better, especially our limits.
3. To understand the present better by giving it a third and maybe a fourth dimension.
4. And then I remind them that when we speak of dementia we first describe memory loss, and that tyrants are generally intent upon rewriting history, or eliminating it, which comes to the same thing.

It seems to me that teachers are apt to pay too little attention to curiosity; they would like us to have a higher, more intellectual, or at least practical reason to learn whatever it is they have been assigned to teach us. Most small mammals that I have had a chance to watch—dogs, cats, chipmunks, squirrels—are intensely curious, more interested in the world around them than they are even in food or sex; their lives would be shorter if they were not so inquisitive. Maybe our own native, burning curiosity has been dampened by living in a world that is too safe, and by having been told too often not to ask so many questions.

To medical students, medicine is symbolized by its technology: the hypodermic needle, the stethoscope, the microscope, the ophthalmoscope (I recall my wonder at being able to see inside the eyeball!), the x-ray, and all the paraphernalia of surgery. The economics of health care, the sociology of disease, even medical biography are acquired tastes for most, but no one passes a display case filled with saws and amputation knives neatly packed in their felt-lined boxes without a shudder and a 100 questions.

Then to discover that not only our colonial forebears used these things, but even the Romans, the Greeks, and long before them the Egyptians and their eastern neighbors in the valley between the rivers, will fire the fertile imaginations of those just beginning to think about the application of steel to living flesh. "What did they do about pain?" What indeed! In Celsus' *De Medicina,*[1] written before the New Testament, we read about how to repair an inguinal hernia:

> . . . and for the day before he must abstain from food; . . . he must lie on his back; next if the groin has to be cut into, and if the pubes is already covered with hair, this is to be shaved off beforehand: and then after stretching the scrotum, so that the skin of the groin is rendered tense, the cut is made below the abdominal cavity, where the membranes below are continuous with the abdominal wall. Now the laying open is to be done boldly (audacter), until the outer tunic . . . is cut through, and the middle tunic reached. When an incision has been made, an opening presents leading deeper. Into this the index finger of the left hand is introduced, in order that by the separation of the intervening little membranes the hernial sac may be freed. . . .

The account goes on in clear, simple Latin sentences, including instructions to take care "lest the abdominal membrane be injured and set up inflammation." There is an admonition to tie the blood vessels, leaving the threads to hang out of the wound, and finally, "Through the margins of the wound itself two pins (fibulae) are then passed, and over this an agglutinating dressing."[1]

Do they picture in their mind's eye this first-century craftsman, this *chirurgus,* slowly working his way through the confusing structures of the groin, repairing an inguinal hernia in a conscious patient, "with a strong and steady hand which never trembles, . . . filled with pity, so that he wishes to cure his patient, yet is not moved by his cries. . . ."[1(297)]

How much of Imperial Rome's GNP was spent on health care might interest some, but not a 22-year-old medical student! "Tell me, what did they do about the pain?"

REFERENCE

1. Celsus, *De Medicina,* 3 vols., ed. and trans. by W. G. Spencer. Loeb Classical Library, Harvard University Press; 1935; 3:401–3.

Connecticut Medicine 1990; 54(7):405

History, Hot and Cold

PHYSICIAN historians jump at the chance to make converts. Every invitation to speak is seized upon as an opportunity to proselytize, to persuade a few more that history is no mere listing of dates and names, but rather that it is a long story of which the present is only the most recent chapter. Not to know what or who came before is like trying to make sense of a novel that we have just opened in the middle, or even more like trying to act in a play, being made to read lines beginning somewhere in the second act.

Some high school students, so we have heard, do not know whether the Civil War came in the first or second half of the 19th century; most medical students, even those from Connecticut, have never heard the name of William Beaumont. A colleague told me that during a recent visit to Vienna, he searched the Allgemeines Krankenhaus and found Semmelweis's First Obstetrical Clinic. He had known about where in that sprawling building to look, and had confirmed the location by finding a plaque on the wall. Some medical students and house officers working nearby had apparently never noticed it; they could not recall having heard of Semmelweis.

The students should not be blamed; it is our responsibility to pass on to them the traditions and the stories of our past. That has always been the duty, as well as the delightful privilege, of the elders in every tribe, to assure the continuity of cultural memory, providing some solid reality to the illusory present. Trying to describe human consciousness may get us caught up in tautologies at worst, and in metaphysics at best; certain it is, however, that without memory there could be no consciousness as we understand it. If we were immediately to forget each present moment when it had passed, we should be automatons; the briefer the memory the more constricted the awareness.

Historical memory must in some way be analogous to individual memory; as it declines, a community, institution, profession, nation, or the entire human race must suffer from a shrinking awareness, a narrowing of consciousness, a decline of wisdom. We store the traces of our past in libraries; traditions, art, and architecture have also carried the record of earlier centuries, but now we are losing our traditions, and buildings are replaced every generation or so. The modern library serves scholars better than ever; in fact, our enhanced ability to store and handle information in nonbibliographic ways has revolutionized the study of history. All the while the diffusion of historical knowledge seems to have declined. Historians write mostly for one another; that kind of exchange among scholars is essential for getting things right, but it hardly adds to historical memory if our students never hear of it.

For history must be told as a story, at least at first: a story that begins in the imaginable past and comes right down to the experienced present. *History* and *story* derive from the same word; in German they are the same word, *Geschichte*. I once heard an historian give a paper, "Some like it hot, some like it cold: two ways for writing history." For students whose business is other than history, it is better hot. The cold "facts" can come later, if the interest is there, and it will be if the tale is well told in the first place. And after the cold facts, the real business of history may get going; the scholar in history tries to come behind the facts, looking for the truth, very much like good novelists and playwrights, who, reversing the order, start with the truth in their heads and present it in the action, the "facts" of the story.

Education, wrote Alfred North Whitehead, must begin with romance, "the half-disclosed and half-hidden possibilities relating Crusoe and the sand and the footprint, and the lonely island secluded from Europe. . . ."[1] To turn students into good amateur historians requires telling a good story with "half-disclosed and half-hidden possibilities," and counting on bright heads to take it from there. For a fortunate few it will be a new road to wisdom—another word, incidentally, which shares by a twisted path a common Indo-European root with *history*.

REFERENCE

1. Whitehead AN: *The Aims of Education and Other Essays*. New York: The MacMillan Company; 1929:28–9.

Connecticut Medicine 1987; 51(11):755

The History Elective

THREE of us have been teaching an elective in the history of medicine for first-year medical students for eight years or so; on the first day we get them to talk about history even though their knowledge, especially of medical history, is remarkably meager. We've gotten used to that: the past is defined for them by great stretches of time called prehistory, the Egyptians, the Greeks and Romans, the Dark Ages, and Modern Times, this last a static period extending backward an indeterminate time to "The War." That limited perspective is not their fault; for most of them their last encounter was a sanitized value-free course in American or European history seven years earlier, mostly forgotten as undoubtedly it should have been.

Our purpose is to let them in on the past, especially medicine's past, so that they can compare and contrast the present with other times and other places, and come to see things that they are just now learning about in ways they might otherwise not be conscious of; to give the flat present a third dimension. History does not explain the present but it tells something about it. Here we get them to talk about purposes, why they are interested in the past, what they expect, and hope, to learn from the course.

By the end of the course each student is required to have done a small piece of original historical research using primary sources. Medical libraries are rich in such materials, since they have journals and old texts, many running back to the beginning of the century or before; our region is full of venerable institutions, archives, and historical libraries. We also want them to learn how to use, or access, the resources of the National Library of Medicine, especially its historical collection, Histline.

Sooner or later in that first session we begin trying to define history: is it everything that was? Or is it limited to the hard evidence of the past, the record, so that everything that happened without leaving a trace is gone forever, as though it had never been? Or is history merely what is written about the past by historians, combining evidence, assumptions, hypotheses, and biases; a kind of literary form, picking and choosing among the remnants to tell an entertaining tale. If so, nothing keeps it from being rewritten every generation or so, recalling George Orwell's lines: "Who controls the past controls the future: who controls the present controls the past."[1]

Is not the past fixed for all time? as the historian G.R. Elton suggests when he writes that historians have an advantage over natural scientists who, in the act of observing nature, change it, and hence can never see things quite as they are.[2(p72)] The past is beyond reach, finished forever; all we can do is describe it, analyze it, draw conclusions from it, but we will never alter it. If history can be altered, and the past not, the two are not synonymous. Students need to recognize that anyone writing history with an objective other than verifiable truth is story-telling at best, spreading dangerous propaganda at worst. This applies even to writing about medical progress.

Because one of us is a real historian, this matter of progress is bound to come up. History is about change, events, and particulars.[2(p21)] Some change is progress, by anyone's measure; no one seriously doubts the advantages of today's medicine over that of 1888, or 1788, at least most of it. But has there been progress in art, music, or literature, or only change? What about politics, the law, education, customs, manners, and ethics? Agriculture, commerce, banking? Better now than then, or merely the ebb and flow of change? And if better, in whose terms, and for whom?

For medical students all of this is a relief from the avalanche of 1980s science that has been falling on them since August, if only they can bridle their anxiety long enough to enjoy it.

REFERENCES

1. Orwell G: *Nineteen Eighty-Four*. New York: Harcourt, Brace and Co.; 1949:35.
2. Elton GR: *The Practice of History*. Glasgow: William Collins & Son, Ltd.; 1968.

Connecticut Medicine 1988; 52(3):185

It Began with the Lensmakers

IT was just 300 years ago this fall that Antonj van Leeuwenhoek, cloth merchant and lensmaker of Delft, using a simple microscope, first described bacteria and recorded what he saw in a letter dated September 16, 1683. He reported seeing individual bacilli as well as clumps and chains in material scraped from the surface of teeth.

Two centuries were to pass before the science of bacteriology would provide firm ground for modern medicine and public health, before Koch would set down the four steps necessary to prove the relationship of a microorganism to a specific disease.

Two of the great discoveries of the 17th century rested upon the work of Dutch lens grinders. Hans Lipperhey had applied to the Count of Nassau for a patent on his telescope in 1608, and, by January 1610, Galileo had seen jagged mountains on the moon, individual stars in the Milky Way, and four satellites rotating around Jupiter. He had obtained a Dutch telescope, modified it with the help of his own lens grinder, whom he initiated to the excitement and danger of the new astronomy, and convinced the Republic of Venice that his instrument had obvious military value, and that to continue he must have the security of a lifetime university appointment.

Antonj Leeuwenhoek's work came more than a generation later; for him lensmaking was an avocation; his career was that of a shopkeeper and cloth merchant. He had used magnifying glasses to inspect cloth, saw their possibilities for scientific work, and set about to learn the art of the lens grinder. He acquired unusual skill in producing minute lenses of outstanding quality. There is one of his lenses in the University Museum of Utrecht which has a magnifying power of 270, and a resolving power of 1.4μ. Some of his observations suggest that he must have made and used lenses of 500 power; it is known that he produced about 550 lenses during the 50 years of his scientific life.

The work of both Galileo and Leeuwenhoek depended upon technology; more precisely upon the perfection of an old technology; optical lenses had been around for centuries. Leeuwenhoek improved upon a simple tool of the cloth merchant; Galileo persuaded his political masters that his telescope would be useful in spotting enemy ships and estimating their firepower. Advances in science sometimes must wait upon the skill of artisans, the inventiveness of mechanics and engineers, and money from political masters. Koch's bacteriology depended in part upon stains developed by the German dye industry; Pasteur's bacteriology was supported in part by the government because of its concern for the French wine and silk industry.

Leeuwenhoek was not only a skilled craftsman; he was a keen observer who discovered and eloquently described—always in Dutch—a whole new world which he had seen through his exquisite little lenses, and he never had to leave Delft to find it. His remarkable descriptions of plankton, blood cells, spermatozoa, and, in 1683, bacilli, comprised the object of his work. His was simply a voyage of joyful discovery, and it sustained his enthusiasm and delighted the citizens of Delft and the Royal Society of London for more than half of his 91 years.

Galileo on the other hand was out to prove a hypothesis; he was disturbed by what Ptolemy's system failed to explain, and he had come to know and accept the ideas of the Polish priest and astronomer, Copernicus. His too was a voyage of discovery; Berthold Brecht has him say to his landlady's young son, "But we're travelling out, Andrea, on a great journey. Because the old time has ended, and there's a new time—I like to think it all began with the ships."[1]

One night when Galileo could find only three of Jupiter's four moons, he surmised that the fourth, had moved behind the planet; that was more than discovery: it was proof that not every body in the heavens turned around the "encapsulated" earth resting motionless in the center of the crystal spheres.

The greatest discoveries are mostly made by looking; the navigators with their ships and the lensmakers with their exquisite glasses gave the "one talent which is death to hide"[2] the tools it needed to launch us upon a voyage of discovery which, 300 years later, has only begun to get underway.

REFERENCES

1. Brecht B: *Leben des Galilei.* Berlin: Suhrkamp Verlag; 1955.
2. Milton J: *On his blindness*; c.1652.

Connecticut Medicine 1983; 47(10):661

How Much Can We Learn from History?

EVERY fall three of us lead a seminar for second-year medical students in the history of medicine. After each session we often conclude that we have learned more than they did. For us the subject is familiar territory; for them it is mostly new ground, and because it is new and they are young, the associations they make and the analogies they draw are often new to us. Last week they read a section from Nancy Siraisi's account of medieval and Renaissance medical practice.[1] They were surprised, as students often are, to find that the Middle Ages were not as violent, ignorant, dismal, and dark as they had always assumed. The readings included some long passages from the time of the Crusades up to the 14th century. One student reminded us that we shouldn't infer too much from these accounts because they were written by and for literate males, mostly in Holy Orders. Another was impressed by, what seemed to her, a remarkably uniform agreement on the purposes and uses of medicine, as revealed in these stories of illness, treatment, and expectations.

The first led us to a discussion about communication gaps between doctors and patients, misunderstandings about treatment, confusion about purposes, and the raising of false hopes, all of which have become more serious problems as medical science has grown more complicated, science literacy has declined, and doctors spend less time with their patients. The other matter, that of objectives, excited a lively discussion. Don't we all understand what medicine is about? And isn't our understanding a common one with our patients and with society?

> To cure sometimes, to relieve often, to comfort always.

Is our goal to make a precise pathophysiological diagnosis, to solve The Riddle, as Sherwin Nuland comments in his *How We Die*? Or is it to treat the patient? And when is the patient not a patient but a subject? What about preventing disease, teen-age pregnancy, gang violence? What about research, especially research on extending life? And what about the insurance companies' interests now that they are increasing their hold on medical practice? What about getting patients out of the hospital as soon as possible to save money? What about putting the profits of the HMO ahead of patient needs? What about marketing to increase the demand for medical care? In whose interest does medicine exist, society's or the individual patient's? Some students admitted that even their goals in medicine might not be as clear as they once believed.

Albert Schweitzer's view of medical care would have much in common with Mother Theresa's but little in common with the view of the surgeon-general or a microbiologist in an academic medical center research laboratory. It's easy to say that they all share the same ultimate goals, but do they, in fact? And anyway, the matter of goals and objectives is management talk. In real life you simply do what comes to hand, solving problems one by one, seeing patients one at a time. One student thought that we should think carefully about objectives before health-care reform becomes an issue again, and suggested that it failed this year because those at the table had their own goals in mind and not those of the patients whom they were supposed to be serving.

The medieval doctor seemed to be concerned with maintaining health, and perhaps thereby staving off disease and death. He was not unaware of the influence of melancholy, fear, and unrequited love on bringing about sickness, and he knew that exercise, diet, rest, and fresh air were important in maintaining health. He did what he could to restore the balance of humors, believing that thereby health would return. He could foretell death fairly accurately when the illness was mortal, but he knew that his means to forestall it were meager.

But the past is a different country, as the students soon recognized; there may be only a few lessons to be learned by exploring it. Science and technology have created a different world, better and braver in some ways, worse and more fearful in others. They were surprised to find that in this dark and superstitious priest-ridden medieval world most disease seemed to be ascribed to natural causes. In a careful study of illness accounts from pre-Crusade Europe, they read that sickness was blamed on sin less than 20% of the time.[2] They concluded that the 20th century was no different, maybe even more inclined to blame the victim. Most admitted that they felt that many patients with drug addiction, alcoholism, lung cancer, chronic lung disease, and AIDS, among others, had only themselves to blame! They tried not to be judges of another's behavior, but they admitted it was not easy.

Like travel, the study of history helps students examine their own surroundings and time, and, as T.S. Eliot wrote, ". . . and know the place for the first time."[3]

REFERENCES

1. Siraisi NG: *Medieval & Early Renaissance Medicine: An Introduction to Knowledge and Practice*. Chicago: The University of Chicago Press; 1990.
2. Kroll J, Bachrach B: Sin and the etiology of disease in pre-Crusade Europe. *J Hist Med Allied Sci* 1986; 41:395–414.
3. Eliot TS: *Little Gidding V*, 1962.

Connecticut Medicine 1994; 58(11):694,697

Section 9—Medical Figures from the Past: Some Favorites

There is properly no history; only biography.

Ralph Waldo Emerson (1803–1882)

All men by nature desire knowledge.

Aristotle (384–322 B.C.)

Osler as Hero

EARLY this fall a small group of senior medical students, called "Scholars in Medicine," met in the home of one of our faculty members to talk about William Osler. One student gave a brief sketch of his life, lingering on some familiar observations on Osler's charm that had been made by his students and residents, his "breezy cheerfulness," and then told of his contributions to medicine, especially to medical education. He read from the Cushing biography and from the 1982 *Principles and Practice*. For the two faculty members this was familiar ground, but we were delighted to fill in here and there with anecdotes, especially some tall tales about Osler's amazing colleague and shadow, Egerton Yorrick Davis.[1]

The discussion of Osler's life and especially the lead he had taken in the development of bedside teaching, went on and on. Students contrasted his ideal of learning in the wards with their own experience of teaching rounds, which often were little more than chart reviews, going over laboratory data and radiology reports, and maybe a quick stop at the patient's door:

> For the third- and fourth-year students, the hospital is the college; for the juniors, the out-patient department and the clinics; for the seniors, the wards. They should be in the hospital as part of its equipment, as an essential part, without which the work cannot be of the best. They should be in it as the place in which alone they can learn the elements of their art and the lessons which will be of service to them when in practice for themselves.[2]

Before this evening none of the students had heard of Osler, except the student who led the discussion and who remarked to me the next day, "I've caught the bug." Seventy years after William Osler's death, those of us who caught the bug 40 or more years ago wonder at his persisting appeal:

> Osler lives today because he was a great clinician, and because he wrote well and collected a great library, and because he had an enduring influence on colleagues and students. But his influence continues strong especially because of his humanism, a quality that resonates clearly with a contemporary resurgence in belief in the importance of humanism in restoring art to today's scientific physician.[3]

That is undoubtedly true, but as I heard these medical students warm to the topic that evening, I sensed that they, some of them, at least, were coming to feel that in this man Osler they might find their hero. They would not have said it that way for hero-worship is out of style; their word would be role model. Here was a man whose qualities, virtues perhaps, of humor, charity, commonsense, and benign humanism, might just be within their grasp. He was no Darwin or Freud to turn the world on its head, no Einstein, had not come close to winning a Nobel [prize], and yet, though he seemed old-fashioned, he was no stranger to the work that was now beginning to fill their lives. During their three years in medical school they had all had their fill of cynical talk about medicine; here was a colleague who, by the example of his life would prove the cynics wrong:

> And lastly, the profession of medicine is distinguished from all others by its *singular beneficence*. It alone does the work of charity in a Jovian and God-like way, dispensing with free hand truly Promethean gifts. . . . We form almost a monopoly or trust in this business. Nobody else comes into active competition with us, certainly not the other learned professions which continue along the old lines.[4]

REFERENCES

1. Tigertt WD: An annotated life of Egerton Yorrick Davis, MD, an intimate of Sir William Osler. *J Hist Med Allied Sci* 1983; 38:259-97.
2. Osler W: The hospital as a college. *Aequanimitas.* Philadelphia: P. Blakiston's Son & Co.; 1904:327–42,341.
3. Roland CG: The palpable Osler: A study in survival. In: Barondess JA, McGovern JP, Roland CG (eds): *The Persisting Osler*. Baltimore: University Park Press; 1985:3–18,17.
4. Osler W: Chauvinism in medicine. *Aequanimitas.* Philadelphia: P. Blakiston's Son & Co.; 1904:277–306.

Connecticut Medicine 1990; 54(11):643

Eponyms and Old Friends

ONE of the many reasons for teaching the history of medicine to medical students is to introduce them to some outstanding men and women they might never otherwise meet; probably they will hear their names, but without a proper introduction they will never know who they were or what they did. They will never remember them.

Not all of their medical forebears will seem especially interesting, perhaps because as students or physicians they will never get to know them well enough; one can hardly get to know everybody. A few might become life-long friends. William Osler may now have more friends and admirers than he had when he was alive; there are Osler clubs and societies all over the English-speaking world. During the Middle Ages Hippocrates and Galen were more widely known than ever in their lifetimes, mostly by admirers rather than by friends.

The marvelous thing about historical people is that each keeps a kind of perpetual open-house. You can visit anytime you like: call on William Harvey or Thomas Browne when you are in the mood for 17th-century England, or Moriz Kaposi or Theodor Billroth if you want to spend an evening in late 19th-century Vienna. While you are there you might, if you can find a copy of his plays, drop in at the Burgtheater for the first performance of otolaryngologist Arthur Schnitzler's new play, *Liebelei*, which opened 9 October 1895 (and was recently presented at the Long Wharf Theater in New Haven under the title, *Dalliance*).

Names in medicine have a way of appearing almost anytime; once they are stored away in long-term memory, an unexpected encounter will evoke a response, and we start off on a reverie, or better yet, a conversation or a search from which we always emerge enriched.

Eponyms are great for that sort of thing; it is unfortunate that we have discouraged their use in medicine, partly, so we say, in the interest of greater clarity or precision, but also partly, I suspect, because we are persuaded that a forward-looking enterprise like medicine has no business wasting time with the past, especially the past of recent memory. A friend, a pathologist and amateur historian, once observed that we are forever discrediting our fathers and rediscovering our grandfathers.

In a few instances we have even failed to recall that an eponym is an eponym. When students with their newfound vocabularies speak of a gram-negative septicemia, not one of them will suspect that Gram was a person, Hans C. J. Gram, a Danish physician who died only a half century ago. I recently mentioned Koch's postulates to a group of students; there was not a flicker of recognition. Most had heard of Louis Pasteur; no one knew anything about Robert Koch or Rudolf Virchow; they had not been introduced. Even Osler's name was unknown to them, and there were uncertainties about Salk and Sabin, Watson and Crick.

Who would ever speak of Osler-Weber-Rendu disease, or Osler's nodes? Even the Babinski reflex has been replaced by the "up-going toe sign," or, if Joseph Babinski's name is used in the write-up, it is generally spelled with a lower case "b!" Last year as we were concluding a second-year session in physical diagnosis, one of the students asked, "Who was Babinski?" That led us into another hour-long search, not only for Babinski, but for other 19th-century neurologists as well: John Hughlings Jackson, Wilhelm Heinrich Erb, Otto Westphal, Pierre Marie, and especially Jean-Martin Charcot. By early evening we had all learned something, and a few of us improved our stores of historical and even clinical knowledge.

If the eponyms all go, these occasions for asking, "I wonder who he was?" will never provide the dessert at the end of an intellectual meal. Teachers of anatomy undoubtedly mention Glisson's capsule, but rarely Bowman's. For curious reasons some eponyms are more durable. Patients are still described as being "cushingoid," a barbarism, and we still hear Cushing's disease and Cushing's syndrome, confused as usual. Recently a colleague and I were searching for our cars in the medical school parking lot, having only the most imperfect recollection of where we had left them that morning. My friend turned to me in exasperation: "I wonder if we're both getting what's-his-name's disease?"

Connecticut Medicine 1987; 51(5):341

Sir Thomas Browne, 1605–1682

IN October, 1905, William Osler gave an address at Guy's Hospital, London, on "Sir Thomas Browne"; he must have planned it to coincide with the 300th anniversary of Browne's birth. This year there will be many addresses memorializing the 300th anniversary of Thomas Browne's death; there will be a service in the Church of St. Peter's Mancroft in Norwich where Browne worshipped and was later buried.

Those of us old enough to have studied from an edition of the *Principles and Practice of Medicine* which includes the preface to the first edition may recall the dedication to "William Arthur Johnson, priest of the parish of Weston, Ontario," the first of three men to whom William Osler dedicated his textbook. Father Johnson was remembered as the teacher who introduced him to the microscope, and who read to his students from Sir Thomas Browne's *Religio Medici*, "in illustration of the beauty of the English language."

Religio Medici was Osler's constant companion in life. His first copy (1862) he called "the most precious book in my library"; later he was to acquire almost all the editions of the *Religio*, including the first one in 1642. Cushing described the scene on the night before the funeral in Christ Church Cathedral, with Osler "—lying in the scarlet gown of Oxford, his bier covered with a plain velvet pall on which lay a single sheaf of lilies and his favorite copy of the 'Religio,' *comes viae vitaeque*."

My first reading of the *Religio Medici* was in the summer of 1937; I found a copy in my father's library, and, while it is neither very old nor of great value, it is indeed precious. Several years ago I purchased a dozen or so paperbacks of the *Religio* to give away, and made one or two converts. Even though it is barely 100 pages in length, his Augustan style requires a leisurely afternoon, and some sections deserve several readings.

Browne's *Religio* was variously received in his own time; although he remained a loyal communicant of the Church of England, rejoiced in the downfall of Cromwell and exulted in the Restoration, he was suspected of popery, skepticism, and even atheism. His fault was tolerance, unusual in the 17th-century when most wars were wars of religion:

> I could never divide my self from any man upon the difference of an opinion, or be angry with his judgment for not agreeing with me in that from which perhaps within a few days I should dissent myself. I have

> no Genius to disputes in Religion, and have often thought it wisdom to decline them, especially upon a disadvantage, or when the cause of Truth might suffer in the weakness of my patronage.[1]

The charitable tolerance of Browne did not rise from indifference in matters of religion. His final lines in the *Religio* express his faith: "—I set no rule or limit to Thy hand or Providence. Dispose of me according to the wisdom of Thy pleasure. Thy will be done, though in my own undoing."[2]

Browne's tolerance is not grim, legalistic, or ideological; rather it is a compound of charity and good nature. Of that latter quality he says, in *Christian Morals*:

> Although their Thoughts may seem too severe, who think that few ill-natur'd Men go to Heaven; yet it may be acknowledged that good-natur'd Persons are best founded for that place;—

Later, in that same discourse, Browne mentions a matter with which we continue to be troubled in medicine:

> With what strift and pains we come into the World we remember not; but 'tis commonly found no easy matter to get out of it. Many have studied to exasperate the ways of Death, but fewer hours have been spent to soften that necessity.

Browne is more than charity and good humor; his philosophy and science illumine a century when the European world was moving from the Middle Ages to the age of science and technology. His language may at times seem obscure to those of us not raised with the notions of neoplatonism in a world of four elements.

Thomas Browne was a successful practicing physician in a time not unlike our own: a century of wars, troubled faith, intolerance, single issues, and grim ideologies. On this 300th anniversary of his death he is worth reading or rereading, if only to try to understand how he managed.

REFERENCES

1. Browne, Sir Thomas: *Religio Medici*, Part I, Section VI
2. Browne, Sir Thomas: *Religio Medici*, Part II. Section XV

Connecticut Medicine 1982; 46(7):415

Benjamin Rush: Doctor and Patriot, 1745–1813

BENJAMIN Rush is so well remembered as a physician signer of the Declaration of Independence that we often forget the four other physicians whose signatures also appeared on that document: Josiah Bartlett, Matthew Thornton, Oliver Wolcott, and Lyman Hall. Wolcott and Hall were Connecticut natives and classmates at Yale, although Hall later emigrated to Georgia, joining the "Puritan Element" in that colony. Oliver Wolcott practiced briefly in Goshen, later was elected governor, and is remembered for being both the son and the father of Connecticut governors.

In a 1787 address Rush encouraged Americans to study the effects not only of America's natural environment but also of its new political and educational institutions on health and longevity:

> It remains yet to be discovered and recorded, whether the extent of human life has been encreased or diminished in America. . . .
>
> It yet remains to ascertain the full influence of cultivation upon our bodies. The highest degrees of it known in America, have had a visible effect upon health. In Connecticut, one of the oldest and best cultivated states in the union, remitting and intermitting fevers are seldom known.[1]

Rush was an Enlightenment man, intelligent, energetic, "sometimes," Garrison wrote, "wrong-headed as well as strong-headed,"[2] zealous in public causes, and intent upon good works. For biographers he has been a complicated subject, deeply religious, a radical reformer, and uncompromising republican; on balance they have not found him wanting. To rely more on system than on experience was quite in keeping with his 18th-century roots: facts were less reliable than reason. He was almost the last of the system-makers, declaring that there was "only one disease in the world"; all disease was hypertension, "a spasm of the extreme arteries." To combat this "morbid excitement" one need only deplete the patient by bleeding and purging. A contemporary, William Cobbett, described Rush's therapeutics as "one of those great discoveries which are made from time to time for the depopulation of the earth."[2]

He worked without rest on behalf of yellow fever patients during the 1793 epidemic in Philadelphia, often visiting more than 100 daily. Some accused him of ending more lives than he saved, but surely he was neither the first nor the last physician to be caught up in false doctrine. When he himself succumbed to the fever, he directed his treatment along the same lines as he had followed for his patients.

His *Syllabus* for his students at the College of Philadelphia was America's first chemistry text; he followed John Morgan as professor of the practice of physic after the Revolution, was chiefly responsible for the Philadelphia Dispensary, and from 1799–1813 was Treasurer of the United States Mint.[3] His monograph, *Medical Inquiries and Observations upon the Diseases of the Mind*, published a year before his death, was an eloquent plea for humane treatment of the insane, ". . . to restore the disjointed or debilitated faculties of the mind of a fellow-creature to their natural order and offices, and to revive in him the knowledge of himself, his family, and his God" (pp. 244–5).

Rush has been described by his enthusiastic admirers as an "American Hippocrates," or an "American Sydenham"; William Osler referred to him often, and commended a biographer for doing "tardy justice to the memory of a great educator and to a public-spirited citizen."[4] Distressed by the long animosity between two old friends and fellow revolutionaries, Rush succeeded in restoring correspondence between Thomas Jefferson and John Adams. His affection for both was great in spite of Jefferson's condemnation of medicine's "fanciful theories":

> I have lived myself to see the disciples of Hoffman, Boerhaave, Stahl, Cullen, and Brown succeed one another like the shifting figures of a magic lantern. . . . The patient, treated on the fashionable theory, sometimes gets well in spite of the medicine. [Letter from Thomas Jefferson to Caspar Wistar, 1807.]

Jefferson's reflection reminds us that very good doctors may be good in spite of their bad theories.

REFERENCES

1. Rush B: *A Discourse Delivered Before the College of Physicians of Philadelphia February 6, 1787 on the Objects of their Institution*. Historical Collections of the Library, College of Physicians. 1987:13–4.
2. Garrison FH: *An Introduction to the History of Medicine* (4th Edition), Philadelphia: W.B. Saunders Company; 1929:378–80.
3. Shryock RH: *Medicine and Society in America, 1660–1860*. New York: New York University Press; 1960:67–81.
4. Osler W: Letter to HG Good, in Cushing's *The Life of Sir William Osler* (2 vol.). London: Oxford University Press; 1926, ii:626.

Connecticut Medicine 1992; 56(4):220

Robert Koch, 1843–1910

> The captain of all these men of death that came against him to take him away, was the Consumption, for it was that that brought him down to the grave.
>
> *John Bunyan (1628–1688)*

ON the evening of March 24, 1882, at the meeting of the Berlin Physiologic Society, Robert Koch delivered an address entitled simply "Uber Tuberculose." The audience, we are told, was spellbound, so moved that there were neither questions nor applause. Paul Ehrlich recalled it as "my greatest scientific event." Koch had incontrovertibly demonstrated that the tubercle bacillus was the causative agent of tuberculosis, a disease at that time responsible for 300 deaths per 100,000 throughout most of Europe and the United States, accounting for one-fourth to one-third of all deaths during the 19th century. A hundred years is not long, less than 2% of historic time. Some of our grandfathers might have remembered the headlines. René and Jean DuBos describe the response:

> The heretofore unseen killer was now visible as a living object, and its assailants at last had a target for their blows. In Europe and America, Koch became the pope of medical science. In Japan, a new shrine was dedicated to him as to a demigod.[1]

His paper, published the next month in the *Berliner klinische Wochenschrift*, contained the first statement of "Koch's postulates"; this was the strategy he had used to prove that the tubercle bacillus was indeed the agent which caused this disease. Only a year before, in their textbook, Austin Flint and William H. Welch had declared their belief in the non-communicability of tuberculosis.

Like so much that is common, tuberculosis received little recognition from medicine during most of the 19th century. Yet, in spite of bleedings and starvings, closed windows and opiates, the death rate had fallen from 500 per 100,000 in 1800 to 150 per 100,000 in 1900. There was less overcrowding and better nutrition in the last half of the century; industrialization had improved the economy in Western Europe and America. Jean Villemin showed in 1865 that tuberculosis could be passed from man to animal and, by repeated inoculation, from animal to animal; it took Koch's photomicrographs, however, to convince physicians that consumption was contagious.

Tuberculosis mortality continued to fall after 1900 to less than one per 100,000 in Massachusetts last year. The decline was not interrupted except for two peaks during the world wars; the introduction 30 years ago of streptomycin, isoniazid, and PAS was barely noticeable on the graphs.

Tuberculosis had been as much a part of the 19th century as Queen Victoria herself. Keats died of consumption at 26; Shelley was in Italy hoping to heal his disease when he drowned sailing his boat, the *Ariel*, at 30. Goethe had a weak chest and coughed blood but lived to 83; Emerson's father died of tuberculosis, and Ralph Waldo and his three brothers all had consumption. Robert Louis Stevenson's creative genius was somehow associated with his tuberculosis, and Thomas Mann's novel, *The Magic Mountain*, was inspired by his visit in 1912 to the sanatorium at Davos where his wife was taking the lung-cure.

Osler, in his textbook, quoted the German axiom, *Jedermann hat am Ende ein bischen Tuberculose*, and indeed almost everyone did have it. In early 19th-century workhouses, most of the children were scrofulous; in my medical school class positive skin reactions exceeded 80%, and three students dropped out because of pulmonary tuberculosis.

Eliminating the "White Plague" from the west is one of medicine's triumphs, yet we still do not know quite how it happened. Koch convinced those who doubted that phthisis was contagious; public health measures clearly had their good effect, but the death rate was already falling. Collapse therapy seemed to hasten recovery, but not until 1952 was there the means in hand to deliver the final blow; by then the job was almost done. Curiously, both Squibb and Hoffmann-LaRoche had brought forth isoniazid at the same time, and then discovered that two German chemists had synthesized it in 1912.

The history of tuberculosis provides a text for many sermons; however, this month should be set aside to honor Robert Koch. He concluded his lucid paper with this affirmation of faith in the fruits of research:

> When the conviction that tuberculosis is an exquisite infectious disease has become firmly established among physicians, the question of an adequate campaign against tuberculosis will certainly come under discussion and it will develop by itself.

REFERENCE

1. DuBos R, DuBos J: *The White Plague*. Boston: Little, Brown & Co.; 1952:102.

Connecticut Medicine 1982; 46(3):163

Virchow's Legacy

RECENTLY a fellow dean who shares with me an interest in the history of medicine asked if we had ever discussed Rudolf Virchow in our seminars. We had, I was happy to tell him, six or seven years ago, invited a fellow from the Johns Hopkins Institute of the History of Medicine to lecture on Virchow's concept of disease as revealed in *Die Cellularpathologie* of 1858. We doubted whether most medical students would have heard his name except in connection with the supraclavicular lymph node sometimes felt in metastatic tumors, rarely in gastric carcinoma, and which, when I was a medical student, everyone called Virchow's node.

In his obituary which was read before the German Pathological Society on September 22, 1902, Virchow was called "the leader of medicine in the 19th century, the reformer of pathology, and a master both of biology and anthropology." It is difficult for us after 83 years to appreciate the extent of the changes in medicine attributable to his work.

The medical reforms which he had in mind as a 25-year-old pathologist in 1846 when he read his paper "Concerning Points of View in Scientific Medicine" were all one with the political and social reforms sweeping over Europe from France in the years just before 1848. His support for "full and unlimited democracy" got him into trouble with his political masters, and he was dismissed from the University of Berlin. His obituary writer referred to yet another claim to fame: "Already as a young pathologist Virchow emphasized the great significance of medicine for human society and called it a social science."

Virchow had grown up in the decades when philosophical systems and mystical romanticism dominated German medicine. The doctrines of *Naturphilosophie* rather than observation and experimentation provided the explanations for natural events, and debates ran on endlessly about whether disease was in the humors or in the solid parts. For Virchow, disease was no interloper seizing possession of the organs or humors but rather "an expression of individual life under unfavorable conditions." Both pathological anatomy and the manifestations of disease were the observable changes arising from *Pathologische Physiologie*.

So also in society, "epidemics must be indicative of major disturbances of mass life." From this came his famous aphorism: "Medicine is a social science, and politics nothing but medicine on a grand scale."

He insisted that cellular pathology was a principle, not a system. So skeptical was he of anything which sounded like dogma that he could never accept the notion that microorganisms could be the sole cause of disease. He did not attend the meeting of the Berlin Physiological Society on the night of March 24, 1882 when Koch presented his conclusive evidence for the bacterial etiology of tuberculosis. Perhaps he adhered too closely to his own concepts, but he has been vindicated in his belief that bacterial agents are but one factor in the causation of disease.

The botanist Matthias Jacob Schleiden had shown that the fundamental unit of plant life was the cell; Theodore Schwann demonstrated the same for animals, thus establishing "one universal principle" for all life. They both believed, however, that cells arose from, were crystalized out of, noncellular material, the cytoblastema.

It remained for Virchow to prove that all tissues, even bone and cartilage, came from cells, and that each cell derived from a preexisting cell, *omnis cellula e cellula*, at least for the higher forms. Not until Pasteur was the controversy over spontaneous generation finally settled.

He returned to Berlin in 1856 and remained until his death in 1902. He continued active in politics first as a member of the Prussian lower house, later in the Reichstag as leader of the opposition; he served for years on the Berlin City Council where he helped to achieve reforms in school health and hospital construction, and was instrumental in cleaning up the water supply and providing for an adequate sewage system. He even took time to help Schliemann in his excavation of Homer's Troy.

For him, medicine was the most encompassing of all the sciences, the unified study of man undertaken to perfect human society—an impossible goal but surely one loftier than the "bottom line" implied in the concept of a health-care industry.

In a recent article, Leon Eisenberg wrote, "Medicine may employ technical means, but it functions normatively for human ends. Assessment of its benefits and its costs must be on social, not technical, grounds."[1] That is the legacy of the great reformer.

REFERENCE

1. Eisenberg L: Rudolf Ludwig Karl Virchow: Where are you now that we need you? *Am J Med* 1984; 77:524–32.

Connecticut Medicine 1985; 49(1):49

Emil von Behring and Diphtheria

A MEMORY from medical school days that still can elicit a sense of dread is that of diphtheria. I recall standing, masked and gowned, at the foot of a narrow bed watching an emergency tracheotomy performed on a "mummied" nine-year-old. I knew that I could never do this, that here was the line that divided the real doctors from the pretenders, and that now was the time to quit while quitting was still possible. Too much for head, heart, and hands to learn, and I was probably not genetically or culturally equipped to practice medicine; after all, as far as I knew, none in my family had been a physician, maybe for good reasons.

Everything about diphtheria had seemed daunting; my own shots of toxin-antitoxin had left a peculiarly vivid memory. I am sure the TAT followed the bad news of a positive Schick. I have a picture-clear memory of our next door family doctor carefully injecting Schick toxin intradermally using an elegant, tiny gold needle which he had just boiled in a spoon over the flame of our gas stove. I recall the red spot on my arm that lasted for days and then peeled. A negative Schick, of course, was required for admission to kindergarten.

Mortality from diphtheria was high even after the general use of antitoxin. At the Herman Kiefer Hospital, the infectious disease hospital in Detroit, overall mortality from diphtheria between 1927 and 1936 was 12.1%, but a little over half the patients had had the mild, tonsillar type. One-fourth of the cases had nasopharyngeal diphtheria and that carried a 30.4% mortality. Hemorrhagic diphtheria, 1.2% of the total, carried a 97% mortality. This was all under nearly ideal conditions and with the proper use of antitoxin. Of course many patients were admitted after several days of croup or sore throat during which no one wanted to think about diphtheria. Prognosis depended on the day of the disease when the antitoxin was first given. And the antitoxin was not without serious risk; serum sensitivity had to be checked for and sometimes the patient desensitized. The epinephrine syringe was always at hand.

If you've read Sinclair Lewis's *Arrowsmith* you may remember Martin's terrifying night in the farmhouse with the little eight-year-old Mary Novak:

> He had to make a decision, irrevocable, perhaps perilous. He would use diphtheria antitoxin. But certainly he could not obtain it from Pete Yeska's in Wheatsylvania.

There followed the wild drive in the old Ford to get the antitoxin, the return, the intravenous injection, then "There was a gurgle, a struggle in which her face blackened, and she was still. . . . Slowly the Novaks began to glower, . . . Slowly they knew the child was gone." And then, as he was driving home through the night, "'I shall never practice medicine again,' he reflected."

It was just a 100 years ago this year that Emil von Behring left the Prussian army to begin his work as an assistant to Koch in the Institute of Infectious Diseases in Berlin. Klebs and Loeffler had identified the bacillus of diphtheria five years earlier, Roux and Yersin at the Pasteur Institute had demonstrated that a sterile filtrate from a diptheria bacillus culture would produce the symptoms of the disease in animals, and in 1890 Fraenkel and Brieger demonstrated that this bacillus-free "toxalbumin" injected into guinea pigs would induce immunity to *C. diphtheriae*. Within days of the report, von Behring had shown that an animal injected with immune serum resisted infection, and an animal with the disease if treated with immune serum could be cured.

The first use of antitoxin in a child with diphtheria was on Christmas night, 1891, in von Bergmann's clinic in Berlin. In 1913 von Behring introduced his toxin-antitoxin mixture for active immunization, but immunization programs were not the rule in North America until the 1920s. Since then mortality rates have fallen from 20 per 100,000 to less than .006.

Emil von Behring shared the Nobel prize with Émile Roux in 1901; his name was among those of the 93 German intellectuals who signed the manifesto against the 1914 war. He died of pneumonia at Marburg, March 31, 1917. Antiserum for that disease, which would cut mortality in half, was still a decade or so away.

Connecticut Medicine 1989; 53(1):59

Pierre Louis and His Numerical Method

PIERRE-Charles-Alexandre Louis (1787–1872) is little known outside medical historical circles; only one of my internist friends knew about his bloodletting study in patients with pneumonia, and a surgeon proudly remembered the angle of Louis, but that turned out to be a different Louis (Antoine). Pierre C.A. Louis belongs to the time before that burst of biomedical science in the second half of the 19th century, the time just after Bichat, Laennec, and Bayle in France, and nearly contemporary with Graves, Stokes, and Bright in Great Britain. Most of us recall names in biology and medicine back through our grandfathers' and even great-grandfathers' generations, but then the mists close in obscuring our vision. The early decades of the 19th century, separated from the Enlightenment by the two revolutions, seem like the early morning hours of our modern world. But this is no place for a historical analysis of the social, cultural, political, scientific, and technical forces that shaped the remarkable European and American 19th century. Historians will be doing that for years to come.

Pierre Louis can claim special honor for his "numerical method" and his requirement for rigorous observation. By impartially collecting facts, carefully recording and analyzing his data using numbers, and following his motto, "Ars medica tota in observationibus," Louis established the foundations of clinical medicine on the firm ground of statistical method. For nearly seven years he lived at the [Hôpital de] la Charité (1820–1827), collecting and analyzing his thousands of observations on typhoid, tuberculosis, yellow fever, and diphtheria. Applying his method to 78 cases of pneumonia, as well as to erysipelas, tonsillitis, and pleurisy, he challenged the efficacy of bloodletting—the mainstay of medical treatment for more than 2,300 years—by showing that it failed to arrest pneumonia at its onset and had little effect on its course.

Louis was the teacher of many Americans, including among others Oliver Wendell Holmes, George Cheyne Shattuck, and H.I. Bowditch. One rainy day in October 1905, William Osler with some American colleagues placed a wreath of autumn leaves on his almost forgotten tomb in the cemetery in Montparnasse to mark ". . . Louis's life which has no parallel in the profession; . . ." and to reaffirm ". . . his special claims to remembrance—not so much his attempt to introduce mathematical accuracy into the study of disease, as his higher claim to have created the American school of clinical medicine through his pupils."[1]

For us Louis's story is a reminder that important clinical questions will be answered only by meticulous, impartial clinical observation, driven by a lively scepticism about most forms of accepted therapy. I recall when we began to doubt the efficacy of dicumerol in the management of myocardial infarction; a cardiologist, beginning to lose his faith, remarked that no one would have the guts to do a serious clinical study. And there are other fashions that have or will follow the way of bloodletting: the Sippy regimen, tonsillectomy, radical mastectomy; everyone has his list of the controversies. How many present orthodoxies, so secure and safe, will fall before 21st-century Louises? The profession had invested heavily in bloodletting; just before Louis, Francois Broussais, the dominant figure in Parisian medicine, was advocating heroic bleeding or leeching for almost all diseases; he was a formidable adversary.

We invest much of ourselves in our orthodoxies, and they are defended by powerful champions, not only in medicine, but among the stockholders and managers of pharmaceutical companies and the investigators whom they support, and among patients who dislike having their habits questioned or faith shaken. To confess that we have been wrong, led on by the fashion of the day, and to explain why, is not easy and is often poorly received.

The recent studies of variations in medical treatment from one place to another have been of intense interest to those whose only goal is to contain costs. These studies ought to be of greater interest to clinicians for they are a kind of superficial updating of Louis's *Researches on the Effects of Bloodletting in Some Inflammatory Diseases*.[2] They ask unambiguous questions that cry out for honest answers.

REFERENCES

1. Cushing H: *The Life of Sir William Osler.* London: Oxford University Press; 1925; 2:20–1.
2. Louis PCA: *Researches on the Effects of Bloodletting in Some Inflammatory Diseases* trans., CG Putnam MD. Boston: Hilliard, Gray, & Company; 1836; reprinted, Birmingham, The Classics of Medicine Library; 1986.

Connecticut Medicine 1989; 53(10):613

The 100th Anniversary of Local Anesthesia

HEARING the story of anesthesiology may begin a lifetime romance with the history of medicine; I remember reading about W.G.T. Morton and John Collins Warren in Logan Glendening's delightful book, *The Human Body*, when I was 12 or 13 years old. The story that was said to end with "Gentleman, this is no humbug," was one of my favorites; there were few dramatic events in literature that could touch those of October 16, 1846, in the Ether Dome of the Massachusetts General Hospital.

In Connecticut, the rival claims of W.G.T. Morton, Horace Wells, and Charles T. Jackson assume the qualities of local legend; both our medical and dental students begin to take sides in the old controversy after they have visited the exhibits at the Hartford Medical Society. Then they read that the Georgia surgeon, Crawford W. Long, had been using ether since 1842. They raise all of the questions about the meaning of priority in discovery and invention, the connection between the spirit of the times and the work of scientists and inventors, the loss and gain that accompany anything new, and, perhaps most important, the human side of scientific discovery, the envy, pride, covetousness, and anger.

Since physical pain, intense and protracted, is the most dreaded of our afflictions, the power to control it safely should have been nearly the most eagerly sought after good of all. The Egyptians and the Greeks used opium perhaps with some effect, and there was alcohol and some other herbs in the long ages of pain which may have helped a little to ease the agony of the knife and saw. But not until the 19th century and the beginnings of the humanitarian movement were two agents, already well known to chemists, employed to prevent pain in the way described by the author of Genesis: "And the Lord caused a deep sleep to fall upon Adam, —."

One hundred years ago, on September 15, 1884, Karl Koller's discovery of local anesthesia was announced at a Convention of German Oculists in Heidelberg; a month later in Vienna he read his paper which described the interest which both he and Sigmund Freud had taken in the alkaloid cocaine. He told of experiments upon animals and then later upon himself, by which he had proved that a 2% solution of cocaine would produce complete anesthesia of the conjunctiva and the cornea for seven to 10 minutes. He reported that foreign bodies could be removed from the eye and operations for pterygium and cataract performed without pain.

Within a month R. J. Hall and William Stewart Halsted, working at Roosevelt Hospital in New York, had demonstrated that the injection of a 4% solution of cocaine around a cutaneous nerve would produce anesthesia throughout the area of distribution of the nerve. Later Halsted injected, by Hall's account, "the inferior dental nerve where it enters the dental canal." The subject, a medical student, developed complete anesthesia of his tongue to the midline, as well as of the gums and teeth on the same side. Halsted repeated that experiment the same evening on Dr. Hall with similar results: the dental and buccal anesthesia was complete for 25 minutes.

The dentists Wells and Morton had given general anesthesia to surgery; a surgeon repaid the debt by giving local anesthesia to dentistry. Discoveries and history are never quite that simple, but ophthalmology and dentistry would surely not have developed as they have without local anesthesia, and surgery would have been stuck in the 18th century without the blessing of general anesthesia.

There was talk of the dangers of frustrating divine purposes and of the salutory effects of pain—always for the other person—and of the moral issue of pain relief in childbirth, talk which has not even yet gone away. In the calculus of loss and gain, anesthesia seems to be mostly gain. Halsted suffered, and so did others, from the unanticipated devastating effects of cocaine; some of those who worked with him even lost their lives, but Halsted, with the help of his colleagues, went on to greatness. According to his biographer, W. G. MacCallum, "the most brilliant of Dr. Halsted's actual discoveries was the conduction anesthesia that he produced by injecting the new found cocaine into a nerve."[1]

REFERENCE

1. MacCallum WG: *William Stewart Halsted*. Baltimore: The Johns Hopkins Press; 1930:239.

Connecticut Medicine 1984; 48(7):475

"Do Not Think, But Try; Be Patient, Be Accurate"

TWO hundred years ago last month Edward Jenner inoculated "a healthy boy, about eight years old," with "matter . . . taken from a sore on the hand of a dairy maid who was infected by her master's cows. . . ." Surely this event marked the beginning of the "modern" period in medical science, the "long 19th century" that was so fruitful in scientific discovery and technologic invention—among many other things. And James Phipps, the boy, and Sarah Nelmes, the dairy maid, were immortalized as few of us will ever be.

Firsts in history are hard to pin down. A Dorsetshire farmer in 1774, using a needle, inoculated his wife and two sons with the cowpox virus. In 1740 a butcher had himself deliberately infected with a needle dipped in cowpox matter. A country practitioner had purposely infected five of seven children with cowpox by having them "handle the udders of infected cows," and observed that they were resistent to subsequent inoculation with the smallpox. Undoubtedly there were others, but to Jenner goes the honor, and for good reason.

When he was a teen-aged apprentice to a physician, Jenner heard a woman say she could not take the smallpox because she had had the cowpox. History, including even medical history, rarely advances by leaps. Continuity is the rule; discontinuities, as saltations in evolution, are singularities.

In first looking into Jenner's wonderful *Inquiry into the Causes and Effects of the Variolae Vaccinae, a Disease Discovered in Some of the Western Counties of England, Particularly Gloustershire, and Known by the Name of Cow Pox* one soon senses that he is standing in the sunset rays of the Enlightenment. Like the Declaration of Independence and the American Constitution, here is late 18th-century prose at its most lucid.

> The deviation of Man from the state in which he was originally placed by Nature seems to have proved him a prolific source of Diseases. From the love of splendor, from indulgences of luxury, and from his fondness for amusement, he has familiarized himself with a great number of animals, which may not originally have been intended for his associates . . . .
>
> In this Dairy Country a great number of Cows are kept, and the office of milking is performed indiscriminately by Men and Maid Servants. One of the former having been appointed to apply dressings to the heels of a horse affected by the Grease, and not paying due attention to cleanli-

> ness, incautiously bears his part in milking the Cows, with some particles of the infestious matter adhering to his fingers. When this is the case . . . a disease is communicated to the Cows, and from the Cows to the Dairy-maids, which spreads through the farm. . . .

Jenner never claimed to be first to inoculate with the cowpox to prevent the smallpox; he *was* the first to reflect deeply on this natural phenomenon that so many had observed, to draw inferences from his observations, to "experiment" and "investigate," his own words, recalling the advice of his mentor John Hunter, "Do not think, but try; be patient, be accurate." He did try, he experimented, and he published his findings in 23 cases to support his assertion "that the Cow-pox protects the human constitution from the infection of the Small-pox."

His work, his vaccination, led to the only eradication of a disease by deliberate intent in history. In the bacteriomania of a 100 years later, many predicted the elimination of all infectious diseases within the lifetime of men and women still living. We are less sanguine now; the invisible world of microorganisms has proven itself well equipped to deal with any strategy we can devise. In fact, mortality from infectious diseases is rising. But there has been no smallpox, anywhere, since 1977.

This was a disease that was known in China 3,000 years ago, that was recognized in Europe as early as the 2nd century, Marcus Aurelius may have died from it (180 AD), it was widespread during the Crusades, and by the 17th century was pandemic in Europe. It entered America with Cortez's troops in 1520 and proved deadly to the Native Americans. In its ravages age and sex, vice and virtue, wealth or poverty made no difference; its scars, pockmarking half the faces in Europe, were seen everywhere from the slums of London to the palace of the royal family. The case mortality rate in America in the 1940s was still what it had been in Elizabethan England—25% to 35%, although the incidence by then, thanks to Jenner and active, progressive departments of health, was no more than 10 to 20 cases per year in most large American cities. Since 1980 it has been declared "extirpated from the earth." By June 30, 1999, all stores of the virus in Russia and the United States will have been destroyed.

Connecticut Medicine 1996; 60(6):365

Metchnikoff's Starfish

Sir Patrick:	That's not new. I've heard this notion that the white corpuscles—what is that what's his name?—Metchnikoff—calls them?
Ridgeon:	Phagocytes.
Sir Patrick:	Aye, phagocytes: yes, yes, yes. Well, I heard this theory that the phagocytes eat up the disease germs years ago: long before you came into fashion. Besides, they don't always eat them.
Ridgeon:	They do when you butter them with opsonin.[1]

ELIE Metchnikoff first observed the phenomenon, which he called *phagocytosis*, in 1883—another centennial event, along with Koch's identification of *Vibrio cholerae*, the deaths of Karl Marx and Richard Wagner, and the first national health insurance law. In some ways the world of 1883 belongs more to us than it does to 1783. You could have felt the 20th century coming in 1883; a hundred years before was another age.

Metchnikoff, son of a Russian guardsman and a Jewish mother, was a zoologist whose sensitive spirit could soar to the heights of optimism and sink to the depths of despair. After the death of his first wife in 1873, he attempted suicide by taking an overdose of morphine. Again, after relinquishing his chair in zoology at the University of Odessa in 1881, he tried again, this time by inoculating himself with relapsing fever.

It was while convalescing in the seaside town of Messina in Sicily that he first observed the phenomenon of *Fresszellen*, "feeding cells." He wrote:

> One lovely day my family had gone to the circus to see some especially well-trained apes. I had remained behind, alone with my microscope, in order to observe the motile cells in transparent starfish larvae; suddenly a thought flashed in my head. These very cells must be useful to the organism in its fight against noxious invaders. Completely filled with the significance of this inspiration, I felt myself terribly excited.

He then went on to tell how he had procured a thorn, stuck it into the Daphne larvae, and observed how it was "quickly surrounded by moving cells." He concluded, "This experiment was the foundation of my theory of phagocytosis to which I was to devote the next 25 years of my life." In another letter, he wrote: "Until then I had been a zoologist; suddenly I became a pathologist."[2]

Immunity was no new concept; as early as 1725, the Reverend Cotton Mather, who followed medicine as well as divinity, had advocated small pox inoculation (not cow pox) during epidemics, and had speculated on the immune process, even including the notion of invading organisms. By 1883, humoral immunity was recognized, but cell-mediated immunity was a new idea.

Elie Metchnikoff was later named director of the Pasteur Institute. In 1908 he shared the Nobel prize with Paul Ehrlich. He died in 1916, a "fanatic of science," Tolstoy called him. Ludwig Aschoff regarded his work, which had led to his own idea of the reticuloendothelial system, as "the most significant in the whole conception of *defensio*, by which term is indicated the reactive process of inflammation."

When his health began to fail, Metchnikoff fixed upon the idea that aging resulted from chronic poisoning by bacteria in the gut, autointoxication, and might be delayed by a diet of sour milk. It was this conviction of his that dominated the medical world; most physicians had never heard of phagocytosis.

In his first textbook, in 1893, Osler mentions autointoxication and almost but not quite dismisses it. He says nothing of Metchnikoff and cellular immunity. By the 10th Edition in 1927, McCrae elaborated:

> Captivated by the theories of Metchnikoff we have been for some years on the crest of a colonic wave, and "intestinal toxaemia" has been held responsible for many of the worst of the ills that flesh is heir to, more particularly arteriosclerosis and old age. The senile and presenile of two continents have been taking some milk and bactobacillary compounds, to the great benefit of the manufacturing chemists.

In 1912, yogurt factories were said to be named for Metchnikoff, and the yogurt market even today may owe a debt to his *poissons intestinaux*. Ideas do not have to be verifiably true to have great durability.

Metchnikoff's real science came from the excitement of discovery, the delight of happy observation. "This is the element that distinguishes applied science from basic," wrote Lewis Thomas, "Surprise is what makes the difference."[3]

REFERENCES

1. Shaw B: *The Doctor's Dilemma*, Act I; 1911.

2. Freund H, Berg A: *Geschichte der Mikroskopie*, Band II, p 233, Umschau Verlag, Frankfurt am Main; 1964.
3. Thomas L: *The Lives of a Cell: Notes of a Biology Watcher*. New York: Viking Press; 1974.

Connecticut Medicine 1983; 47(5):305

Section 10—Books and Reading

Some books are to be read only in parts; others are to be read, but not curiously; and some few to be read wholly, and with diligence and attention.

Francis Bacon (1561–1626)

Books like friends, should be few and well-chosen.

Samuel Johnson (1709–1784)

No Requirements, Please!

AFTER finding a new book or discovering an old one, some friend or colleague is often anxious to tell me that every medical student should be required to read it. Except for making it a requirement, I generally agree. Most of us could make a list of works which physicians should read; our lists would not be the same, and we should probably find that we had read only a handful of those on anyone's list, even our own. Osler had his list of 10 which he called a bedside library which included the Bible and all of Shakespeare, but he left out Dante, most of the poets, and all of the moderns except Holmes.

When someone declares that a book or play should be required reading for medical students, he must believe that the author has come upon some new truth that physicians especially ought to know. Perhaps in his experience doctors are blind to that truth, and he is persuaded that their patients would benefit if that blindness could only be removed. In most people's view physicians know a great number of facts about science and technology, but neglect other kinds of truth, or may have neither the wit nor the time for them.

That is an old reproach, and portrayals of physicians as single-minded technicians hiding behind incomprehensible systems are as ancient as any literary tradition. George Bernard Shaw's *The Doctor's Dilemma* is one of the better modern works on this theme. Of course, every medical student ought to read it! Shaw called it a tragedy, and whether the tragedy is medicine's failure to achieve greatness even with the help of modern science, or the moral decline of Sir Colenso Ridgeon, or the unmoving death of the artist, Louis Dubedat, is up to the reader to decide.

There are doctors in books and books by doctors; there is more in novels about medicine and society than the sociologists have dreamed of. There is more written about sickness and death than about doctors, and in all these stories there are truths that cannot be expressed as well, or even expressed at all, in the language of science. Although psychiatrists may have known this, the behavioral scientists seem often about to discover what Chaucer thought everyone knew.

While some things we know by immediate experience, most of what we know, or will ever learn, is by analogy, by relating a new observation to an older experience, by imagining a story. "Then began he to speak to the people this parable" (Luke 20:9). There are finespun psychological and literary theories about the place of myth in understanding the world, and obscure philosophical theories about the relation of illusion to reality. Fortunately we do not have to comprehend these to enjoy a good tale or to be grateful to the author for showing us a new truth. Whether creativity in the writer is different from creativity in the scientist is less important to know than that each has a special and equally authentic understanding of the truth. Matthew Arnold made the observation that if the aim is "to know ourselves and the world, we have, as the means to this end, to know the best which has been thought and said in the world." He later explained that his phrase encompassed science, literature, and art.[1]

Arthur Schnitzler, the turn-of-the-century Viennese otolaryngologist, wrote *Novellen* and plays with a deceptively light touch, which nevertheless showed his full understanding of the theories of his friend Sigmund Freud. In *Sterben*, the story of a young writer dying of tuberculosis, there is acceptance and denial, grief and rage, which we only recently have discovered about death and dying. There is a specialist who feels compelled by the patient to tell the truth: "I must have certainty"; a physician-friend who wants desperately to share in his patient's delusions of ultimate recovery; and there is a hint of the doctor's dilemma, although Schnitzler's *Novelle* is 20 years earlier than Shaw's play. Every medical student ought to read it! And then follow it with Thomas Mann's *Magic Mountain*. And then Chekhov. The list grows longer; a lifetime is not enough to come to the end of it.

REFERENCE

1. Arnold M: *Literature and Science*. Rede Lecture; 1882.

Connecticut Medicine 1979; 43(2):112

William Osler: Humanist

THE American Osler Society will meet, appropriately, in Montreal this year to celebrate the sesquicentennial year of the great physician's birth, July 12,1849. It is old style, I know, and politically incorrect, misguided, even gauche to attribute greatness to anyone in these enlightened times, most especially to a white, European male. Perhaps Caucasian would be a better word than white to use for William Osler: the painter of the famous "Four Doctors," John Singer Sargent, spoke of him as "This little brown man. I don't know what to do with him. I have never painted a man with an olive green complexion." Osler himself, wrote of Sargent's famous painting, "He has caught my eyes and the ochrous hue of my dour face. . . ."[1]

One of Osler's admirers, Edith Giddings Reid, titled her 1931 biography *The Great Physician*; the work is an encomium, a panegyric, almost too much even for those of us for whom WO remains a hero in these days when all are equal and when, for most, every hero has become "a bore at last." When Dr. Henry Sigerist, hardly a political conservative (although he would surely have balked at political correctness), published *The Great Doctors* in that same year (in German, *Die Große Ärzte*; the English translation came out in 1933), he ended it with William Osler, the final biographical sketch in a series of 48 that began with the physician-architect Imhotep (2900 B.C.). Sir William was the only North American among Sigerist's greats, undoubtedly reflecting his continental point of view before he moved from Leipzig to Baltimore:

> What gave the man so widespread an influence was that, in contradistinction to so many of the noted European clinicians of that day, he was no mere one-sided man of science. Although he did more than anyone else to introduce precise laboratory methods into the field of American clinical medicine, he was a born humanist. He loved books, collected them, and read them by the score.

Indeed Osler collected books, bound volumes, including incunabula, and manuscripts to a total of more than 7,700 in all, now catalogued and annotated in the *Bibliotheca Osleriana* and resting securely on the shelves of the Osler Library at McGill University. In his life of 70 years this man taught students "at the bedside" at four universities, McGill University, University of Pennsylvania, John Hopkins, and Oxford University, wrote textbooks, essays, histories, biographies (his bibliography includes 1,473 separate titles), lectured all over North America and Europe, practiced medicine, counting "all sorts and conditions of men" among his patients, and yet was recognized as a humanist scholarly enough to be elected president of the Classical Association of Oxford.

In his presidential address to that association in May 1919, seven months before his death, Osler spoke of the natural synergy that ought to exist between science and the humanities. One paragraph struck me as apt for our time, 80 years later:

> The extraordinary development of modern science may be her undoing. Specialism, now a necessity, has fragmented the specialties themselves in a way that makes the outlook hazardous. The workers lose all sense of proportion in a maze of minutiae. Everywhere men are in small coteries intensely absorbed in studies of great interest, but of very limited scope. . . . Applying themselves early to research, men get into the backwaters far from the mainstream. They quickly lose the sense of proportion, become hypercritical, and the smaller the field, the greater the tendency to megalocephaly.

Osler's final words in that address bear repeating:

> There is a sentence in the writings of the Father of Medicine upon which all commentators have lingered, 'For where there is love of man, there is also love of the art'—the love of humanity associated with the love of his craft!—philanthropia and philotechnica—the joy of working joined in each one to a true love of his brother. Memorable sentence indeed! in which for the first time was coined the word *philanthropy*, and conveying the subtle suggestion that perhaps in this combination the longings of humanity may find their solution, and Wisdom—philosophia—at last be justified of her children.

When our class graduated from medical school 53 years ago, Eli Lilly & Co. gave each of us a copy of Osler's *Æquanimitas*. I believe many of us read it through, in fits and starts, during our internship year. At an earlier urging of our professor of medicine, many of us had already acquired and even read Harvey Cushing's prize winning *Life of Sir William Osler*. Some even acquired and promised ourselves to read at least some of his "Bed-side Library for Medical Students":

I. Old and New Testament
II. Shakespeare
III. Montaigne
IV. Plutarch's *Lives*
V. Marcus Aurelius

VI. Epictetus
VII. *Religio Medici*
VIII. *Don Quixote*
IX. Emerson
X. Oliver Wendell Holmes—*Breakfast Table Series*

Some medical students are still drawn by Osler's magic, but fewer, I believe, each year. His language is Old Western and to most must now seem archaic. Those of our colleagues born after World War II have rarely heard it spoken, have almost never read it. The allusions, subtle and often hidden, mostly escape them; they know little of Greek and Roman authors; and not much of Shakespeare, the Bible, and the 18th- and 19th-century poets and novelists, that our teachers took so seriously. And medical history before DNA, AIDS, and CABGs, is a blur, largely irrelevant, a strange place. Social historians, vaguely Marxist, and humanists who expend their talents in deconstructing texts have rendered liberal education in these latter decades, except for the sciences, mostly unnoteworthy, unappealing, a waste of time. Is the remedy in Osler's bed-side library? I doubt it; with three or four exceptions, his list today would swamp the hardiest. But his advice that precedes it is worth considering:

> Well filled though the day may be with appointed tasks, . . . rest not satisfied with this professional training, but try to get the education, if not of a scholar, at least of a gentleman. Before going to sleep, read for half an hour. . . .

Efforts to recover the old humanities have been made by restorationists in our century. The University of Chicago and its Great Books curriculum, St. Johns in Baltimore and Santa Fe with its mandatory two years of Greek and French and the classics in science and philosophy have been brave efforts to revitalize the roots of Western civilization, but they started no revolutionary movements in higher education.

Interest in great literature (another politically incorrect sin: aren't all texts of equal value once they are deconstructed?) begins in adolescence. What we read in American Lit and English Lit in high school 60 years ago appealed to most of us, helped us tame the surging hormones, suggested modesty, romance, and civility, and, I believe, made a difference. The titles I recall, beyond a fairly deep immersion in English and American poetry, included among others Shakespeare's *Julius Caesar, The Taming of the Shrew, Hamlet, Macbeth,* and *Romeo and Juliet;* Dickens's *David Copperfield, Oliver Twist,* and *A Tale of Two Cities;* Stevenson's *Treasure Island*, and Scott's

Ivanhoe. Current literature was mostly neglected—almost nothing later than 1914, but there were movies that whetted the appetite for more. And no television! And of course no PCs!

Osler's formal classical education stopped after he entered the University of Toronto: a year of theology, and then medical school, and yet he is remembered as a humanist, one in the style of his own heroes, Dr. Thomas Linacre, Sir Thomas Browne, Sir Thomas More.

Sometime in the 1960s medical schools began to reintroduce medical history into their curricula, and often integrated it with literature and medical ethics. Humanistic Studies in Medicine it was called at the University of Connecticut. Several of us who attended a meeting of the Congress on Medical Education in Chicago in the late 1960s or early 1970s took seriously a remark made by Edmund Pellegrino to the effect that "Medicine is the most humane of the sciences and the most scientific of the humanities." We also had begun to suggest that premedical students meet only the minimum requirements for science—they would get plenty of science in medical school— and devote the remainder of their undergraduate education to the humanities.

There is little evidence that the humanities in medical education, including even medical ethics and medical history, will make our students better doctors, more compassionate, empathetic, or clinically skillful—their characters are settled long before the medical school years—but it may make for a deeper understanding of life's mysteries, maybe even better judgment. To the student he [Osler] wrote:

> There are great lessons to be learned from Job and David, from Isaiah and St. Paul. Taught by Shakespeare you may take your moral and intellectual measure with precision. . . .
>
> Begin at once the cultivation of some interest other than the professional. . . . When tired of anatomy refresh your minds with Oliver Wendell Holmes; after a worrying subject in physiology, turn to the great idealists, to Shelley or to Keats, for consolation; when chemistry distresses your soul, seek peace in the great pacifier Shakespeare; 10 minutes with Montaigne will lighten the burden.

Such advice can't harm, and since our work with patients usually begins with trying to understand a brief autobiography or biography, we become unwittingly literary critics anyway.

Connecticut Medicine 1999; 63(3):175–6

Summer Reading

"IF one cannot drive, one can read," wrote David Broder in his column last month. Being set free from the tyranny of the automobile for some of our days does give us time for other pleasures and pastimes.

Summer is an especially good time for reading, *and* although reading while loafing needs no purpose beyond the mere pleasure of it, I suspect one could say that it is as beneficial to health as jogging, there being no data to support the efficacy of either. For physicians I recommend medical history.

Oswei Temkin, former director of the Institute for the History of Medicine at The Johns Hopkins University, makes a distinction between the *past*, "everything that happened," and *history*, "the past organized into a tale."[1] He designates the serious study of history, including research and explanation, as *historiography*. For those of us who are busy with practice and trying to improve our art and science, history as the "past organized into a tale" is enough, especially if it is a good tale. Serious scholarship might come later, but it doesn't have to.

In anxious times of rapid change and gasoline shortages, the longer view which history provides can have a settling effect, and may even add wisdom to the business of making sense of the morning newspaper. No one reads history deliberately to gain new perspectives or some grand world view. History interests us because it is, if artfully written, a good tale, often a tale of people we have known, of places and times in which we have lived, and of scenes in which we may have played some part.

Medical history and history of science are again respectable academic disciplines. The number of serious scholars in these fields has increased tenfold in the past decade. If this is anything more than a passing academic fancy, it could signal something momentous in our western culture. One of the discoveries of the Renaissance was that Europe had had a past; only in this century have we been producing graduates who, like students in the12th century, are unaware of any time before their own.

Because the present moves on with such speed, even the recent past is soon forgotten. Benson and McCallie[2] recently reviewed five treatments for angina pectoris which had been advocated with enthusiasm during the past 50 years, and then abandoned. With each new treatment 80% of the patients were improved, but that percentage fell rapidly with subsequent trials, until now all of these treatments have been abandoned. Three of the treatments were drugs: xanthines, khellin and vitamin E; two were surgical procedures: ligation of the internal mammary artery and implantation of the internal mammary artery. Without adding a single new "fact," this bit of medical history helps to put coronary artery bypass in a context where it assumes a new meaning, much like putting a word in a sentence.

These new insights are useful and momentarily exciting; they are not the chief reason for reading medical history for those of us who will never become medical historiographers. There need be no other justification than the pleasure that one may attach to any harmless avocation.

For me a vertical approach to reading history is more satisfying than a horizontal one: one century, one person, or one disease at a time. The 17th century is good to start with; it is that part of the late Renaissance when science was getting underway, and it is a good century from which to launch into the Middle Ages or even into classical times. Chauvois' *William Harvey*[3] is shorter and easier to read than Geoffrey Keynes' biography, but for an introduction into the way a 17th-century physician might solve a biological problem, Harvey's *De Motu Cordis* is preeminent and can be read in a weekend. For an understanding of how a classically educated young physician from the same time thought about religion and philosophy, Thomas Browne's *Religio Medici* makes another weekend project. Together they are a fair excursion to that great century, and the commentaries on Browne and Harvey which are available in any good medical library could easily usurp all leisure reading for a year.

For some this will all seem to be dullness and irrelevancy. But for others a door might open into a new room whose fascinating crannies can be explored without using much money or gasoline. If you are a Dorothy Sayers fan, you may remember that Lord Peter Wimsey carried Browne's *Religio Medici* in his inside coat pocket. That would be ideal for gasoline lines.

REFERENCES

1. Temkin O: *The Double Face of Janus*. Baltimore: The Johns Hopkins University Press; 1977:6.
2. Benson H, McCallie DP: Angina pectoris and the placebo effect. *N Engl J Med* 1979; 300:1424–28.
3. Chauvois L: *William Harvey*. New York: Philosophical Library; 1957.

Connecticut Medicine 1979; 43(8):525

Doctor Stories

FOUR or five decades ago when my colleagues and I were 30-somethings, new members in a growing group practice, our Saturday parties generally fell into a predictable pattern; after the first drink we left our wives in the living room talking about the kids and drifted into the kitchen where the liquor was plentiful, and told doctor stories until the small hours. "Don't you guys ever talk about anything but medicine?"

"What else is there?" we might have said, but didn't. The truth was that we never could resist the temptation. No one mentioned politics, the weather, baseball, or religion—just medicine of the "I had a patient" kind.

In those days I was seldom home for dinner before seven o'clock; my wife accused me of just not being able to leave the hospital. She recited the line from *Wind in the Willows:* "Believe me, my young friend, there is nothing—absolutely nothing—half so much worth doing as simply messing about in boats." Only she said "hospitals," and I had to agree. Some of the hospital time was taken up by doctor talk also, but qualitatively different from the more imaginative 1:30 AM kitchen talk.

In the dedication to his book, *The Human Body* (1927), Logan Clendening recalls to an old friend, Peter Thomas Bohan, how "we have shown one another many pathological specimens, ensconced temporarily to the horror of our respective wives, in our respective bathtubs, and we have sat over many a mug of grog far into many nights discussing battle, murder, and sudden death." He hopes "that we may both long be preserved to indulge these relatively innocent pastimes, . . ."

Forty or 50 years ago books of doctor stories, mostly autobiographical, enjoyed a considerable popularity: Arthur Hertzler's *The Horse and Buggy Doctor* (1938), Gordon Seagrave's *Burma Surgeon* (1943), Walter Alvarez's *Nervousness, Indigestion, and Pain* (1943), and later, *Incurable Physician* (1963), and more recently, Lewis Thomas's *The Youngest Science: Notes of a Biology Watcher* (1983), and Francis D. Moore's *A Miracle and a Privilege* (1995). As medicine became less clinical and more reductionist after World War II, I suspect that much of the popularity of this genre among nonmedical readers began to wane. Even for doctors calcium channels seemed less appealing than real hearts in real patients!

The Lost Art of Healing, by Bernard Lown, MD, (1996) is one of the most recent doctor books, and should have a good sale. He writes of the older clinical era of first-half 20th-century medicine, while telling of the remarkable advances in cardiology after 1950. The narrative is sustained by wonderful doctor stories of the "I had a patient" kind. Dr. Lown and his mentor, Samuel A. Levine, MD, are the chief personae, who demonstrate over and over the diagnostic and healing power of the history and physical examination, of the time spent with the patient, listening, touching, understanding, and making friends. I am saddened when I hear students in our introductory clerkships being told to take "focused" histories and do limited physical examinations based on the chief complaint. Those of Dr. Lown's and my generation long ago learned that the chief complaint is only the ticket for admission; it takes thoughtful, sympathetic listening and questioning to uncover the answer to our question, "What brings you in to see me today?" After a careful history and thorough examination, we should have the answer; a few tests should confirm the diagnosis. Lown makes short work of the excuse that a battery of blood tests, x-ray examinations, imaging, and catheterizations are just smart, defensive medicine; rather they offer false promises of certainty; more than that, they are lucrative, and sometimes dangerous. An example is the indiscriminate use of the Swan-Ganz catheter:

> I return to my central thesis. Our health care system is breaking down because the medical profession has been shifting its focus away from healing, which begins with listening to the patient. The reasons for this shift include a romance with mindless technology, which is embraced in large measure as a means for maximizing income (pp. 156–7).

His doctor stories are best of all. Some stretch credulity, as when Dr. Levine diagnosed a developing massive anterior myocardial infarct by laying the palm of his hand over the precordium. Not only his sense of touch, but all of his other clinical senses were at work as well! Anyway, when we tell stories, especially stories about ourselves, some refining and altering is always called for. The poet Andrew Hudgins was right: ". . . autobiography dances on the shifting middle ground between fact and fiction, reportage and imagination, actuality and art. . . ."

Connecticut Medicine 1997; 61(1):49

Section 11—A Potpourri

It is almost the definition of a gentleman to say that he is one who never inflicts pain.

John Henry, Cardinal Newman (1801–1890)

So throw off the bowlines. Sail away from the safe harbor. Catch the trade winds in your sails. Explore. Discover. Dream.

Mark Twain (1835–1910)

Leisure, an Antidote for Phrenitis

FRENETIC (or *phrenetic*, as the British spell it) carries with it a sense of mad or insane activity, even though it is often used with pride to describe a burst of healthy industry. Occasionally a colleague tells me of the "frenetic pace of his work this past year," or the word slips into the minutes of a busy committee; it has been used to describe an intern's life, or the bustle of an academic health center. It may be the best adjective to apply to life in the late 20th century.

Frenetic shares its etymology with *frantic*, both coming early into the language from the Greek *phrenitikos*, which means someone with *phrenitis*, or inflammation of the brain and its coverings. In all of its older usages, in English and in other languages, it connotes craziness, madness, or delirium. There may be some sense of the visionary or enthusiast, but not much.

Perhaps our century, in comparison with others, is afflicted with a kind of madness. Information which four generations ago traveled no faster than the speed of a running horse, now moves with the speed of light in amounts and in detail inconceivable even to my father in his youth. Information calls forth response, in turn generating new conditions which insist upon new responses; related to the *phrenitis* there seems to be a diminishing capacity to select which information to attend to and which responses to make. You can almost feel the synapses heating up and burning out.

Individuals, institutions, and governments exchange information and decisions so rapidly that responses are only half-completed and pile up unfinished on one another before they can get out. Is the analogy to a beehive that has just been thwacked with a broom handle, or to a colony responding to the dance of worker bees who have just discovered a vast field of alfalfa? Are we buzzing frenetically or shouting with joy?

In the academic medical center of the last century life's pace was slower. The telephone was not ubiquitous; beepers were unheard of; the computer and photocopiers were mercifully far in the future, and traveling more than two hundred miles called for careful preparation and the luxury of uncomplicated time.

William Osler described his schedule for writing his textbook in the years between 1890 and 1892. He began work on *Principles and Practice of Medicine* after a summer abroad, *four months* of leisurely travel, a *Studien-*

reise, which included stops in Freiburg, Basel, Zurich, Munich, Oberammergau and the Passion Play, Heidelberg, Paris, London, Berlin, and a meeting in Washington before returning home to Baltimore in September. He called it his "quinquennial braindusting," and knew that it was necessary for ending or beginning any great enterprise. It was January before he "got well into harness:"

> Three mornings of each week I stayed at home and dictated from 8 AM to 1 PM. On alternate days I dictated after the morning hospital visit, beginning about 11:30 AM. The spare hours of the afternoon were devoted to correction and reference work—The routine there was:—8 AM to 1 PM dictation; 2 PM visit to the private patients and special cases in the wards, after which revision, etc. After 5 PM I saw my outside cases; dinner at the club about 6:30, loafed until 9:30, bed at 10 PM, up at 7 AM.[1]

Here was no *phrenitis*. Compared with how most of us spend our days, this would seem like cloistered peace.

"The best test of the quality of a civilization is the quality of its leisure," Irwin Edman writes at the beginning of his essay, "On American Leisure,"[2] and later describes leisure as "those pauses in our lives when experience is a fusion of stimulation and repose. Genuine leisure yields at once a feeling of vividness and a sense of peace. It consists of moments so clear and pleasant in themselves that one might wish they were eternal." To understand leisure is to know that it is "an affair of mood and atmosphere rather than simply of the clock." I think that Osler was writing of work and leisure together, of working leisure or leisurely work, which may be important if work is to be creative, and I believe he was describing something not so very uncommon in the 19th century. Even work with leisure called for interludes of loafing. From the same century, in some golden summer, Walt Whitman wrote:

> I loafe and invite my soul,
> I lean and loafe at my ease observing
> a spear of summer grass.[3]

REFERENCES

1. Harvey AM, McKusick VA: Introduction, *Osler's Textbook Revisited.* New York: Appleton-Century-Crofts; 1967.
2. Edman I: *The Uses of Philosophy*. New York: Simon & Schuster; 1955:116.
3. Whitman W: *Song of Myself.* 1855.

Connecticut Medicine 1978; 42(8):541

Intemperance or Intelligence?

> Either men will think that the nature of gout is wholly mysterious and incomprehensible, or that a man like myself who has suffered from it 34 years, must be of a slow and sluggish disposition not to have discovered something respecting the nature and treatment of a disease so peculiarly his own.

THOMAS Sydenham was 59 when he published his "short tract upon the Gout and Dropsy," in 1683. He continued:

> Gout attacks such old men as, after passing the best part of their life in ease and comfort, indulging freely in high living, wine and other generous drinks, at length, from inactivity, the usual attendant of advanced life, have left off altogether the bodily exercises of their youth.

Disease as punishment for the sins of gluttony, wrath, and lust is an ancient theme; the rational 18th century saw it more as the natural consequence of intemperance. Although the hereditary nature of gout had long been suspected, overindulgence and venery, especially for those in mature years, were considered to predispose to its attacks. Anger has more often been associated with sudden death, and Osler wrote of John Hunter's saying "that his life was in the hands of any rascal who chose to annoy and tease him." In his monograph *Angina Pectoris* (1897), Osler gave an account of Hunter's death:

> As he had himself predicted, death came suddenly, in consequence of a fit of temper at a meeting of the governors of St. George's Hospital, October 16, 1793. When contradicted flatly, he left the board room in silent rage, and in the next room gave a deep groan and fell down dead.

Luxuria, ira, and *gula*, lust, wrath, and gluttony, the first three of the seven deadly sins, are by some called the warm-hearted or disreputable sins. By contrast, the other four, covetousness, envy, sloth, and pride are cold-hearted and respectable. It is the first three with their excess of hot humors which are dangerous to health; the faddish concern with "life style" and how it may cause both sickness and health is nothing new.

James Cadogan in his *Dissertation on the Gout*, written 81 years after Sydenham's Tract, repeats the theme:

> Whatever doubts may be entertained of moral evils, the natural, for the most part, such as bodily infirmity, sickness, and pain; all that class

> of complaints which the learned call chronic diseases, we most undoubtedly bring upon ourselves by our own indulgences, excesses, or mistaken habits of life; or by suffering our ill-conducted passions to lead us astray or disturb our peace of mind.

Horace Walpole suffered his first attack of gout at 38 and documented 34 more attacks before he died at the age of 80. He knew of its hereditary nature, but had learned from Cadogan that intemperance, along with indolence and vexation were the true culprits; in a letter to George Montagu he wrote:

> If either my father or mother had had it, I should not dislike it so much; I am herald enough to approve if it descended geneologically—but it is an absolute upstart in me. . . . They tell me of wine to keep it out of my stomach—but I will starve temperance itself—I will be virtuous indeed; that is I will stick to virtue, tho' I find it is not its own reward.

A century after Cadogan, William Osler in his 1892 *Textbook* advises that "Alcohol in all forms should be avoided," and later, "Gout, in many cases, is evidence of an overfed, overworked, and consequently clogged machine."

Though gouty ancestors and disreputable sins make a risky combination, the suspicion lingers that gout has about it something of respectability and worth. Tuberculosis was the romantic malady of poets and artists; the successful men of affairs were gouty. "It is a disease of the higher classes," wrote Osler and 75 years later James Wyngaarden continued and enlarged upon this pleasing notion:[1]

> . . . Formerly a sign of intemperate living, it is today a hallmark of superior intelligence and academic or executive success. Medical students—will be reassured that they are statistically well represented within the hyperuricemic group.

REFERENCE

1. Wyngaarden, JB: In: *Osler's Textbook Revisited.* New York: Appleton-Century-Crofts; 1967:178.

Connecticut Medicine 1982; 46(9):555

Selective Memories a Half Century Old

FIFTY years ago this month I graduated from medical school. So did 6,200 of us in that final war-time class that had finished four years of medical education in 36 months. Internships began the first of April 1946 and ended June 30, 1947—15 months which was our great good fortune. For many in that class this would be the end of their graduate medical education; residency positions nationwide were open to only about two-thirds of that group. Most had to defer further postgraduate training anyway until 1949 in order to serve their mandatory two years in the service.

The war had ended eight months earlier and most of the younger full-time hospital staff were out of uniform and back at work, full of new ideas and quite clearly taking over the place from those who had been too old, in their late 50s and early 60s, to go off to another war. The Henry Ford Hospital in Detroit was jumping with new technology. Penicillin had mostly replaced sulfadiazine and type-specific rabbit serum in the treatment of pneumonia, and streptomycin and para-aminosalicylic acid (PAS) were being used in the tuberculosis (TB) ward. A new division of infectious diseases was created in the department of medicine.

I had to relearn how to digitalize a patient: no longer 16 to 20 grains of digitalis leaf divided in the first 24 hours, 1 to 2 grains daily thereafter, but rather 1.2 milligrams of digitoxin to start, and 0.1–0.15 milligrams daily. Morphine was still ordered in apothecaries' units, 1/4 or 1/6 grain, but demerol came in milligram doses, barbiturates, aspirin, and aminophyllin in grains, and mercuhydrin in milligrams [sic]. An Addisonian crisis was treated with whole ox adrenal extract IV and desoxycorticosterone in oil intramuscularly. The laboratory still reported serum potassium and sodium in milligrams percent, although the flame photometer came into use that year, and soon we were thinking in milliquivalents, and worrying about fluid and electrolyte balance, thanks to the pediatricians.

A young pediatric cardiologist had been sent off to Johns Hopkins to work with Helen Taussig and to learn how to catheterize hearts. Sometime that summer as a medical intern I was tolerated in the operating room as Conrad Lam (Yale Medicine Class 1932) performed the first Blalock-Taussig operation in Michigan on a young girl for tetralogy of Fallot. Incidentally, two years later Dr. Lam put together the first artificial kidney in Michigan, fabricating it from the parts of an Easy washing machine. It worked.

About that same time ball-point pens appeared on the market for $18, the per diem charge for a private hospital room! My wife and I had had our order in for a new postwar Chevrolet for months; these were the first ones out since ‘42, and ours arrived in November 1946. The cost, $1,040, seemed unbelievably expensive for a Chevrolet; a standard Chevy had been only about $600 before the War. Our car was a virtual singularity, a ‘46 GM car, in a staff parking lot filled with Fords, Mercurys, and Lincolns, mostly prewar—the “Ford Fine Family of Cars.”

Medical and nursing care was excellent and equal in quality throughout the hospital, but there were clearly four tiers of amenities: African-American, colored was the word then used, motor plant workers and compensation cases, the large middle class, and the Grosse Pointe or Palmer Woods crowd admitted to the gold coast, B2, where tea was served from a teacart in the afternoon, and a favored few, members of the Ford family, Walter Reuther, a supreme court justice, and others of like rank, might even have spiritus fermenti oz. ii to iv ac [before] the evening meal. Racial segregation had been slowly loosening its hold in the hospital, especially since the 1943 riots and the increasing numbers of black workers in the auto plants during the War. More and more middle-class African-Americans were admitted to hospital floors other than the M3 unit to which they had typically been assigned.

In the TB unit, M2, we learned to initiate and refill pneumothoraxes (or is it pneumothoraces?), check our results fluoroscopically, and follow with interest and more than a little skepticism the few patients who were receiving streptomycin and PAS. In the long winter afternoons during the TB rotation, while the patients slept, or pretended to, I read, stretched out in an old Edwardian leather-upholstered reclining chair. Medical journals, of course, but I do recall some of the books I read that month after finishing the *New England Journal*: John Hersey’s *A Bell for Adano*, Arthur Hertzler’s *The Horse and Buggy Doctor*, Blaise Pascal’s *Pensées*, and John Henry Newman’s *Apologia pro Vita Sua*. The house staff organized and presented the cases for the weekly chest conferences and we learned about the indications for phrenics, pneumos, and thoracoplasty when all else failed.

It was at a Friday morning medical grand rounds that I heard Dr. Frank Sladen, the physician-in-chief, refer to hospitals, such as the Henry Ford Hospital, as public trusts whose sole reason for being was to serve the sick; he said we must never forget that. He also urged the economical use of the laboratory, reminding us that three blood chemistries might equal a salesclerk's weekly wage. My first presentation involved a case of typhus; I still have the notes in which I attempted to explain the Weil-Felix reaction, and read a few paragraphs from Hans Zinsser's *Rats, Lice, and History*.

Lunch was served in two elegant dining rooms. A private one for the medical staff, another for the housestaff, with residents sitting at tables for four, and interns at one long table, all with spotless linen, real napkins, ice water pitchers, and the best salt rolls I've ever tasted. We could bring our wives or a guest on holidays and Sundays. Absolutely no smoking, there or anywhere in the hospital or on the grounds, until after Mr. Ford died in 1947, and even then lighting up was furtive, usually out on one of the porches or on the roof.

We got our haircuts in the hospital barber shop, and our cars serviced and washed in the hospital garage! I bought Ford coke, produced at the Dearborn plant, for our furnace at home. We got our medical and dental care there and even did our banking at the branch in the hospital lobby.

We failed to appreciate how much we were learning by being privileged to watch diseases from beginning to end. Nationally the average hospital length of stay in the mid 1940s was 14 days. We saw untreated Graves' disease melt under sedation and Lugol's solution. We recorded the patient's course, aided by an occasional basal metabolic rate (BMR), until the surgeon, internist, and house staff all agreed that tomorrow was the day for the subtotal thyroidectomy, to steal the thyroid! Hospitalization for serious illnesses like hyperthyroidism was for at least a month, and even longer for patients with ulcerative colitis, rheumatoid flare-ups, rheumatic fever, and acute myocardial infarction. This last involved oxygen by tent (a liquid oxygen tent invented at the hospital in the 1930s), morphine, and then barbiturate sedation, and complete bed rest for 10 days, no radio, no newspaper, no visitors except immediate family, and, for alternate admissions, dicumerol with daily prothrombin times. We were part of a multi-institutional study. The intern examined a centrifuged urine sample daily for red blood cells. The patient might "dangle" after two weeks, but never go home until the seventh week. Lots of time to get acquainted, time to learn the course of disease and its effect on the family, time to form friendships with the patients and have long conversation with families.

Medical interns were required to serve one month on the psychiatric unit, Fl, an open ward modeled on the inpatient units of the Phipps Clinic at Hopkins. Dr. Thomas Heldt, the psychiatrist-in-chief who had trained under Adolf Meyer, made rounds vested in a white coat, as did all other staff physicians and residents, a stethoscope and reflex hammer in his pocket, and a little bag with a blood pressure cuff, ophthalmoscope, and assorted neurologist's paraphernalia. Like all staff physicians at the hospital, he dictated his progress notes to the intern after seeing each patient. He also checked all of the intern's physical examination findings, and made sure that sinus, dental films, and occasionally a Graham-Cole series (cholecystogram) had been ordered to check for foci of infection. Following rounds came electroshock-therapy rounds, and occasionally the administration of insulin for the induction of hypoglycemic shock. Some patients underwent a two-week amytal sleep—*Dauerschlaf*, after which they were placed for a day or two on a mattress and bedding on the floor and "reconstructed" their personalities! Since the psychiatric floor was an open unit, the nurses and housestaff needed some effective controls in cases of patient misbehavior; in the nurses' station were a firehose, very strong orderlies, and a syringe available loaded with apomorphine.

The two most frequent medical emergencies were acute pulmonary edema and diabetic ketoacidosis. Interns did the admission blood counts and urines, sputum smears for acid-fast bacilli or pneumococcus typing, if indicated, and stool guaiacs. We drew all the blood specimens for the laboratory every morning with the help of a good nurse and an elegant, well-equipped cart made in the hospital shop. This job had to be finished in time for resident's rounds at 8:00. Residents or interns started all IVs and gave all intramuscular injections—mostly penicillin—every three hours around the clock. We even learned to sharpen needles!

Otherwise the pace was leisurely, the hospital corridors quiet, and throughout a sense that everything was terribly efficient and spotlessly clean. The head floor nurse was a hierarch without a trace of democracy in her soul. We learned more in those 15 months than ever before or since, and the friendships formed have lasted, except for deaths, half a century. Reflecting on these 50 years only confirms my long-held notion: real progress is rare and by lucky chance; rather what we experience mostly are changes and tradeoffs, and always uncertainty about how the books will balance in the end, uncertainty about the unintended effects of theories and therapies that looked so reasonable and good at the time. It seems to me, looking back, that trust, confidence, and respect abounded between doctors and patients, doctors and doctors, doctors and nurses. Though the hospital hierarchy was real and well defined it was also eminently civil, all intended "for the benefit of the sick."

Connecticut Medicine 1996; 60(3):181–2

The Amazing Atomic Keyboard

MENDELEEV'S Periodic Table was almost my first encounter with the strangely rational nature of science. I can still see that big yellowish, shiny chart hanging in our high school chemistry lab, the 92 elements arranged in orderly octaves with their atomic weights and numbers in the upper-left and lower-right hand corners of each of their boxes. I wondered who Mendeleev was, and how he ever figured the thing out. It was only after we learned that atoms resembled tiny solar systems with electrons all spinning about a central sun or nucleus of protons and neutrons, that the table began to make sense. My father, who was a physicist and head of the science department, had explained most of that to me before, but it had seemed too impossible; how can you know these things if you can't see an atom?

Two other mysteries had plagued me, neither having much to do with chemistry and its Periodic Table. I recall watching the slow emergence of leaves from their buds in early spring. I wondered how the cells, dividing as the leaf grew, knew right where to stop at the edge to form the patterns of the maple leaf or the elm, always knowing exactly how to line up, making a pattern they could never see.

And the third mystery: after learning to play pool at a friend's house, I suppose I was 10 or 11, I observed that the tangent at which one ball struck another determined exactly the direction each ball would take after the impact. It came to me that all causes and effects must be that way, atoms bumping atoms, the results invariable, *a* always causing *b* and then *c* and so on. Nothing random. That being so, how could I choose to play pool with my friend rather than to go skating? The chain of causes and effects from the beginning of the universe must be precisely as they are, fixed, completely determined. Free will, the power to choose, was surely an illusion. The whole thing, everything, had been settled *ab initio* when the universe began! I had not yet heard of Heisenberg and his indeterminacy principle, although that hardly solves the problem!

That was too much for me, so I decided to reserve my wonder and amazement exclusively for the Periodic Table. To me the elucidation of a periodicity in the nature of the elements, then 92, lined up by atomic weight, was a beautiful affair. I have since learned a little more about the Russian chemist, Dmitri Ivanovich Mendeleev (or Mendeleef, or Mendeléeff, or Mendeléyev), who was one of three chemists in the 1860s who observed that many of the properties of elements arranged according to their atomic weights recurred in octaves. The other two were John Newlands, an Englishman, and Lothar Meyer, a German, but Mendeleev gets the credit for the Table as we know it. He claimed the whole thing had come to him in a dream, just as Kekulé saw the solution to the benzene ring problem in a daydream of snakes swallowing their tails. The sequence of atomic weights had actually been noted first by an English physician, William Prout, who in 1815 observed that the atomic weights of the known elements seemed to be integer multiples of the atomic weight of hydrogen. Exceptions existed; we recall chlorine, for example, with its atomic weight of 35.46, too far off to be a mistake, and later explained by assuming mixtures of isotopes.

The clinical neurologist Oliver Sacks recently described his more impressive encounter with the Periodic Table when he was 12 years old, a precocious kid who already knew about the "families" of elements, the alkali metals, alkaline earth metals, the halogens, the inert gases, and so on. The Table he first saw was mounted on the wall of the Science Museum in London. It was a giant wooden cabinet "with 90-odd cubicles each inscribed with the name, the atomic weight, and the chemical symbol of the element."[1] In each cubicle was a sample of the element, at least of those that could be seen at room temperatures and were, I am sure, not radioactive.

Back in the 1940s, my father's cardiologist prescribed LiC1 as a salt substitute for him to use to relieve the dullness of his low-salt diet. That seemed sensible to me; lithium was just above sodium in the Table. I thought he probably could have used KC1 just as well. Of course, today potassium chloride is marketed as "No Salt." These were the first three alkali metals in Group 1. I had once seen metallic sodium, I can't remember where, but I hoped that someone someday could chill a sample of hydrogen down to near absolute zero to see if that most prevalent of elements in the universe had the shiny look of a metal! I think I recall an article in *Science* years ago in which that was reported, but that may have been a daydream!

I used to wonder whether molecules in which silicon was substituted for carbon, as in SiO_2, and H_2SiO_3, could, under strange extraterrestrial conditions as yet unimagined, build compounds analogous to those in organic life on this planet. There are a few, such as triethyl silicol, that are true alcohols. But silicon is incapable of forming complex chains as carbon does so magnificently. Amorphous silicon is a brown powder, and the crystals are grey. Somehow perhaps analogous to lamp black and diamonds?

The beautifully simple little planetary systems of the almost mechanical Bohr atomic model were beginning to fade even in high school textbooks of the 1930s when I first learned about the Periodic Law, though I still draw them that way when I am showing someone, usually a grandchild, what H_2O really looks like. Since 1964 those solid elementary particles, the neutrons and protons, have seemed less solid. Each now is known to consist of three quarks with spins and colors and flavors, all far beyond my comprehension. And quantum theory tells us that these particles—electrons, quarks, positrons—are both waves and particles. And as for spinning about a nucleus of neutrons and protons, Erwin Schrödinger, the inventor of wave mechanics, wrote only that they "do something."

Recalling his early fascination with the Periodic Table, Oliver Sacks wrote:

> The periodic table was incredibly beautiful, the most beautiful thing I had ever seen. I could never really analyze what I meant here by beauty—simplicity? coherence? rhythm? inevitability? Or perhaps it was the symmetry, the comprehensives of every element firmly locked into its place, with no gaps, no exceptions, everything implying everything else.[1]

When Mendeleev, Newlands, and Meyer stumbled upon the recurring similarities in elements arranged by atomic weights in the 1860s, the Periodic Law had absolutely no theoretical basis; they had no idea of the Thomson-Rutherford-Bohr model of the atom with its nucleus and electrons hovering about it "doing something." That was a half century away. By 1913 quantum mechanics was providing a simple and natural explanation for what had been empirical observations.

An analogy exists in biology. At about the same time that Gregor Mendel's observations on inheritance were being made, Dmitri Mendeleev was demonstrating the remarkable periodicity of characteristics in chemical elements. But Mendel's observations, like Mendeleev's, had no theoretical basis. Mendel's publication was neglected until the first years of the 20th century, being finally recognized at about the same time as Max Planck announced his quantum theory. The discovery of the chromosomes in the 1880s revealed something of the machinery of heredity, but not until 1953, when Francis Crick and James Watson published their article in *Nature* on the "Molecular Structure of Nucleic Acids," was the mechanism made clear. The 19th century was truly a most fertile garden for scientific discovery.

REFERENCE

1. Sacks O: Mendeleev's garden. *Am Scholar* 2001; 70:21–37.

Connecticut Medicine 2001; 65(12):741–2

Acknowledgements

I WOULD like to thank all those who participated with me in preparing this collection of essays from the writings of the late Dr. Robert U. Massey.

Permission to reproduce these essays was granted by *Connecticut Medicine: The Journal of the Connecticut State Medical Society* and by Matthew C. Katz, Executive Vice President of the Connecticut State Medical Society.

Dr. Massey's family was most gracious in supporting this project, with special thanks due to his daughter, Janet Massey, for her helpful comments.

I particularly would like to thank Sherwin B. Nuland, MD—surgeon, author, Lecturer in Yale College, Fellow of the Institution for Social and Policy Studies at Yale University, and a close and long-standing friend of Dr. Massey's—for the deeply felt and eloquent foreword he wrote.

Colleagues of Dr. Massey at the University of Connecticut School of Medicine—Ralph Arcari, PhD, Assistant Professor in the Department of Community Medicine and Healthcare, and David Gillon, Associate Dean for Finance and Administration—offered many valuable suggestions. H. David Crombie, MD, retired Clinical Professor of Surgery at the medical school and the current editor of *Connecticut Medicine*, wrote a biographical sketch of his predecessor at the Journal and gave advice and wise counsel from the start of this project, for which I am extremely grateful.

I especially want to express my gratitude to Wanda E. Jacques-Gill, the managing editor of *Connecticut Medicine*, who wholeheartedly brought her talents and skills to this undertaking. It was a pleasure working with her.

Grants from the University of Connecticut Foundation, Inc. and the Sadow Family Education Enrichment Fund made this anthology possible. It also enjoys the encouragement and support of Cato Laurencin, MD, PhD, Dean of the School of Medicine and Vice President for Health Affairs, and Peter J. Deckers, MD, Dean Emeritus, University of Connecticut School of Medicine.

The guidance of Richard Altschuler, the publisher of Gordian Knot Books, kept me on a steady course and was most appreciated.

Again, my sincerest thanks to everyone who helped in putting this book together. The enthusiasm with which all participated was, in my mind, a measure of the profound respect, admiration, and warm feelings felt for the author of these essays—Robert U. Massey.

Martin Duke, MD

Robert U. Massey, MD
A Biographical Sketch

ROBERT Unruh Massey was born in Detroit, February 23, 1922, and died in Avon, Connecticut on February 5, 2008. His father was a science teacher and the director of science education for the Detroit school system. Bob became interested in writing while editor of his high-school paper and class yearbook and an editor of his college newspaper in Oberlin College. It was during this latter period that he met June Collins, a violin major, at the Oberlin Conservatory. Bob entered medical school at the University of Michigan, and in 1943, after his first year, he and June were married.

Bob transferred to Wayne State University School of Medicine and graduated in 1946, cum laude and AOA. Completing postgraduate training at Henry Ford Hospital in 1950, he took a position at the Lovelace Clinic in Albuquerque, New Mexico, where for 18 years, interrupted only by a two-year tour in the U.S. Army, he served as Director of Medical Education and Chief of Medicine, was involved with aerospace medicine, and helped establish the University of New Mexico School of Medicine.

In 1968, Dr. Massey was recruited to join the new medical school at the University of Connecticut. He contributed to the Connecticut community for the following 40 years as physician, writer, editor, classical scholar, historian, mentor, and dean of the medical school (1971–1985). His founding of the Department of Community Medicine with emphasis in ethics, humanities, and medical history, coupled with his efforts at forming a consortium of regional hospitals for education and patient care, were high points of his deanship. The Robert U. Massey Auditorium and the Robert U. Massey History of Medicine Society at the medical school are named in his honor.

After retiring from his medical school responsibilities. Dr. Massey was editor of the *Journal of Medicine and Allied Sciences* (1987–1991) and of *Connecticut Medicine* (1986–1998). His essays in the latter journal were admired and were notable for their expressions of scholarship, wisdom and reverence for the profession of medicine in the tradition of his hero, Sir William Osler.

Dr. Massey's final years, though saddened by the loss of his son and his wife, were inspiring to all for his demonstrated kindness, love, avoidance of rancor and self-pity, and true devotion to other human beings and to medicine that had so characterized his life.

H. David Crombie, MD

Robert U. Massey, MD
1922–2008

CPSIA information can be obtained at www.ICGtesting.com
Printed in the USA
BVOW032359290412

288896BV00004B/1/P